WINDSURFING

The Skills of the Game

D1412498

WINDSURFING

The Skills of the Game

BEN OAKLEY

THE CROWOOD PRESS

First published in 1987 by
The Crowood Press Ltd
Ramsbury, Marlborough
Wiltshire SN8 2HR

Paperback edition 1988
Revised edition 1994

British Library Cataloguing-in-Publication Data

A catalogue record for this book is available from the British
Library.

ISBN 1 85223 830 5

Acknowledgements

The author would like to thank Jane Clague for her assistance in
rewriting parts of the text.

Front cover photograph: A very serious looking Peter Hart
cranking a gybe in Barbados, courtesy of Alex Williams. Back
cover: Nathalie Lelievre (F12) on her way to winning one of the
Indoor Windsurfing events at Bercy, Paris, courtesy of Phil
Jones.

Other photos supplied by: Tony Dallimore, Cliff Webb, Caryl
Sprinzel, Stuart Sawyer, the PBA and the author.

Throughout this book the pronouns 'he', 'him' and 'his' have
been used inclusively, and are intended to apply to both men
and women. It is important in sport, as elsewhere, that
women and men should have equal status and equal
opportunities.

Typeset by Phoenix Typesetting, Ilkley, West Yorkshire.
Printed in Great Britain by Redwood Books, Trowbridge,
Wiltshire.

Contents

Ben Oakley was a top international competitor and is now the RYA National Coach. In 1985 he won the overall Heavyweight category at the Mistral World Championships. Then after qualifying as a teacher from Cambridge University he was appointed RYA Funboard Trainer, alongside Peter Hart, responsible for training the highest qualified instructors. His extensive coaching experience includes acting as visiting coach to the Chinese Olympic Team and instructing in Israel and Barbados. He attended both the 1988 and 1992 Olympic Games as British coach, and numerous youth championships with the British U19 Teams.

He is a regular contributor to the windsurfing press and has written articles for *The Times* and the *Observer*.

With windsurfing being such a young sport, Ben is one of the first top coaches to emerge who has sampled all aspects of it.

His book is clear and concise, and not only are his technical explanations flawless but he also offers sound practical advice on a number of issues, including how you can best approach practising each skill.

Even in his successful competition years Ben took an active interest in coaching, and he was one of my instructors on a training week in 1983. Books cannot substitute for a personal coach, but I am sure Ben's approach to improving your technique expressed in this book will help every windsurfer who reads it.

Mark Woods
World Production Funboard Champion 1986–87

Ben is one of the most experienced windsurfers in Great Britain, and his record speaks for itself. Furthermore, he is one of our top coaches whose understanding of the sport is thorough and whose skills at conveying the relevant ideas have been proven at all levels.

I am delighted that he has at last written a book of this type. It is the first comprehensive book to be produced by a top windsurfer who also has a wide coaching experience. It is unique in that it draws together the whole RYA teaching scheme from beginner to advanced, with an additional excellent chapter on competitive windsurfing. The layout is clear, with some superb diagrams to illustrate the finer points. The opening chapter, in particular, takes a different approach and should be read by all those serious about improving their windsurfing at whatever level.

I am sure this will become a work to which many instructors and sailors turn for useful hints and tips.

Phil Jones
RYA National Boardsailing Coach

Approaches to Learning

As you will discover, I am very much a believer that we largely teach ourselves when learning new skills and that the main purpose of a book or instructor is to help clarify exactly what your aims are. This book, rather than simply telling you how to execute a manoeuvre, suggests valuable methods you can use to practise more efficiently. The book closely follows the graded teaching system of the Royal Yachting Association (RYA) and it is no coincidence that the chapters use the names of the RYA's Levels 1 to 5.

Many windsurfing texts that aim to make you a better sailor explain the skills and techniques you need to master in a 'how to do it' format, with numerous photographic sequences of the manoeuvres involved. What they don't spend much time on is the way in which you are supposed to *approach* learning the new skills. This opening chapter uses a slightly different method and looks at the greatest variable in improving – namely ourselves – since the way we approach and react to learning greatly affects the end result.

THE INNER GAME

In recent years far more attention has been paid to psychological factors in skill development, the catalyst being the book *The Inner Game of Tennis* by Timothy Gallwey (Cape, 1975). It became the best selling tennis book ever and has affected the competitive approach and attitudes of a number of sportsmen. Three years later a highly successful 'Inner Skiing' book was also published.

The inner game approach rests on the belief that the correct technique can and does develop naturally and painlessly given the opportunity and the right environment. Our bodies can learn to respond to new situations if trusted to learn how for themselves. Take, for example, learning to ride a bike, which in fact is quite a complex skill. No one ever teaches you how to ride – you are given the opportunity with stabilisers and encouragement, with the right environment being a smooth, safe pavement. Through trial and error and careful practice the body learns how to balance, pedal and steer all at the same time.

Gallwey describes this learning process in detail by referring to a 'Self 1' and a 'Self 2'. The instinctive way of doing something, the bike riding part of us, is the characteristic of Self 2. As you age, though, analytical thought plays its part and this is personified in Self 1: the voice that reminds you when you play tennis that you must relax, must follow through, must win the point, must play well because your father is watching, and invariably provokes nervous tension and interrupts the instinctive natural flow.

Because of the disruptive influence of Self 1 on our performance, Gallwey, rather than teaching us how to perform a skill, concentrates on ways of distracting Self 1, thereby letting the body perform in its own intuitive way. In tennis he will ask his students to call out their estimate of the height of the ball above the net as it crosses from side to side, or he will ask them to shout 'Bounce' each time the ball bounces and 'Hit' each time it is hit, giving Self 2 a chance to show what a fluent player he really is.

The Role of Instruction

An 'Inner Windsurfing' approach has yet to be fully developed, but we can benefit by using some of the ideas and assumptions. Take, for instance, the idea of a Self 2 which could instinctively teach itself to windsurf like riding a bike. Clearly at a basic level if you just gave someone a board and lake to practise on, apart from being dangerous it would take many months of frustration for them to work out what to do. The best way to learn is to attend an RYA school where, with good instruction and a safe environment, you can pick up the basics in a day or two. Provided the basic technique is sound, which is one of the aims of RYA recognised schools, rapid improvement can be made by letting the body teach itself. Indeed, almost all top windsurfers are self-taught.

The role of books such as this and instructors beyond a basic level is to set out clearly the aims for learning. It is ridiculous to suggest that a magazine article, book or even the most expert of instructors can teach you exactly how to perform the complex set of movements involved in, say, gybing. They can show

you what you are aiming at by breaking down the manoeuvre and showing the role of each movement, but putting it all together with correct co-ordination and timing is up to you to teach yourself. Instructions should help to clarify what you have to do and what factors are involved, but the timing of each movement is self-taught.

Later in the book, I shall describe different skills and manoeuvres, explaining what I think are the important factors for success. The aim of this chapter is to show that you are often your own worst enemy when learning new skills, but with a little understanding, teaching yourself can be quite productive.

Obstacles to Learning

Fear, anxiety, tension, whatever you care to call it, is a common hindrance in all sports requiring balance and results in a loss of commitment and an awkward rigidity in stance; movement becomes restricted and everything becomes more difficult to do.

People often have an underlying fear about falling in and dislike not being in complete control. Confronting and accepting the reason for the tension is often the best way of dealing with it, since if you look logically at the cause it is often not as bad as the imagination suggests. After all, water is the most forgiving of mediums to fall into – and falling in is part of the fun!

ENVIRONMENT
The environment you choose to learn in plays a crucial role in how well you progress. At a windsurfing school the environment is carefully chosen to be safe and suitable for quick progress, with the

wind being the only variable. Unfortunately the weather conditions often prevent you from learning gradually, unlike a ski slope where you can choose the degree of difficulty of each individual run.

Your decision as to *where* you sail is very important. One of the reasons I managed to improve so quickly was that I practised in flat water with a steady wind. Having perfected each manoeuvre on the flat water, I could then sail down the estuary to the open sea and practise what I had learned on the waves. Too many people do not think about where would be best to sail and invariably head straight for the coast in an effort to make progress. Sea conditions are often very choppy, particularly at high tide with an onshore wind which makes sailing well very difficult. On the sea you inevitably feel more unsafe than on flat water and this, combined with the knowledge that many onlookers are watching your sailing, produces an environment ill suited to learning. Furthermore, on the coast there tend to be some expert sailors around and your confidence in your own ability does not benefit from comparison with them.

CONFIDENCE IN THE EQUIPMENT

Another aspect that interferes with learning is not having confidence in the equipment. The old adage that a bad workman always blames his tools is borne out on many a windsurfing beach. It is far easier to blame equipment for failure than oneself. When a person is reluctant to trust his board and sail as designed, then awkward movements are bound to follow. The top brands, such as Mistral, benefit from such thinking since some people are prepared to pay high prices to 'buy' confidence in their equipment.

Fig 1 Experimenting is a good way to improve. However, when practising always sail in a safe, flat water environment and never venture underneath any diving boards.

PRACTICE

Of all the obstacles to learning, perhaps the greatest is the way in which we approach practice. In spite of a keen desire to reach greater heights, progress is hindered by poor practice methods which make improvement slow and frustrating.

In *Sail, Race and Win* (Macmillan, 1982), Eric Twiname uses the analogy of his piano playing compared to that of his young concert pianist friend to illustrate this important point. The young concert pianist had spent fewer hours reaching concert standard than he had spent achieving a mediocre amateur level. The greatest difference, however, was not in

9

the length of practice but the approach to it: he struggled at it whilst she didn't. He went all out at a new piece, rushing into it with lots of enthusiasm and wrong notes, trying to make it sound like the finished piece as soon as possible. The concert pianist did exactly the opposite. Rather than taking the piece as a whole, she broke it down into smaller parts and then worked on them with separate hands and at varied rhythms. Individual difficulties would be singled out for special treatment: 'When a passage went wrong during practice, she didn't mentally beat herself with a stick and get angry, merely went over it again, maybe more slowly, or homed in on the particular difficulty that had tripped her up and worked on that.' This clearly illustrates that the way you approach practice greatly affects how much you improve, irrespective of talent.

SELF-COACHING

What we must do is appoint ourselves as our own coach since, as we mentioned earlier, ultimately we teach ourselves. The idea of self-coaching is not to turn your windsurfing into a strict coaching regime and take the fun out of it, rather to be a little more honest with yourself and let the coach part of you analyse and objectively observe what you do. All this involves is a slightly different approach to your windsurfing. The basic idea is to break down manoeuvres into smaller component parts, concentrating on polishing up each part in the sequence before considering the whole.

The following ideas may help to make your practice more fruitful. Throughout, the carve gybe (a high speed, fairly advanced manoeuvre) is used as an example.

Knowing your Level

The first thing to recognise is at what level you are currently performing. Unfortunately, with funboards people tend to classify their level by the type of board they sail rather than how well they sail it. All too often people have a board with footstraps, so they assume they should be doing funboard manoeuvres, such as the carve gybe. On many occasions I have been exasperated by people who can't even use a harness or sail consistently in strong winds attempting these manoeuvres. Without good stance, harness use and upwind ability, you will never be able to spend enough time on the water before tiring.

The RYA's grading system will help to solve this problem. You can use the table of course contents of the National Windsurfing Scheme (see Appendix) to judge your own level. The carve gybe appears as one of the manoeuvres of Level 4, so before attempting to carve gybe you should be able to do all the material in the preceding levels. Try to be honest with your use of the table and don't attempt to run before you can walk.

The Reaching Trap

For many beginners reaching, turning and often falling is what an afternoon's windsurfing consists of, which, although it is comforting and fun to be with the dozens of others who are doing exactly the same, doesn't lead to much improvement in their sailing. Just as you should carefully select your sailing venue, so you should also think about the type of sailing you do.

The trouble with reaching all day long is that there are no aims to your sailing.

Before launching, it is worth setting your-self some objectives. An obvious one might be to execute three good carve gybes. Instead of doing the usual reach–fall–reach, choose a point a few hundred metres upwind as a target to sail to, then you can concentrate solely on gybing as you work your way back down-wind. This way you learn how to sail upwind, don't have to worry about drift-ing too far downwind in the gybes and have plenty of water space in which to practise without sailors speeding past. You also have a distinct end to the prac-tice when you reach the point from which you set out. Another aim might be to see how far upwind you can sail in ten min-utes, trying to beat it each time you do it.

Experimentation

A further way of introducing some pur-pose to a day's sailing is to experiment with different ways of doing things, since you can only be sure that you have found the best way by deliberately trying differ-ent ways. There are so many variables involved in sailing a board that the experi-mentation can never stop. You could, for instance, try differing lengths of harness lines or changing the amount of weight you place on each foot. The best results come from working with someone else with whom you can sail and discuss the findings.

Experimentation was the method that I used to learn the carve gybe. I can vividly remember trying all sorts of feet positions before deciding which one worked best, then I concentrated on the upper body. Wondering what would happen, I tried pulling up on the boom as I went into the turn. After a few attempts I found that I was turning like Robby Naish for the first part of the turn, then falling in on the inside of the turn. So, with this result, I decided to try the opposite by pushing down on the boom through the turn. The next few gybes were the first I had ever done with speed all the way through the turn; in fact it happened so quickly that I couldn't change the rig fast enough – so then I had to work on the rig change. The significant point is that you have to split a manoeuvre up and experiment with each part for practice to be worth while.

POST-MORTEM
Experimentation is wasted unless you stop to analyse the results of it. At the end of a day's sailing it is worth thinking about what you have learned that day, and try-ing to work out why the new technique works better than the one it has replaced. To do this you will need some knowledge of windsurfing theory.

In my gybe, it seemed that by pulling up on the boom I was committing a lot of weight to the back which, although turn-ing the board initially, caused it to lose speed through the turn. By pushing down on the boom I was keeping the rig more upright, hence providing more power whilst also keeping the board more level and stopping the back of the board dig-ging in too much.

Copying

OBSERVATION
By watching and sailing with someone of a higher standard, you can pick up small points about better positioning and the way they approach a manoeuvre. Everything happens so quickly on the water, though, that all you are left with is a vague impression, particularly with something like the carve gybe.

11

Perhaps the greatest value lies in studying pictures of an expert doing a manoeuvre, since from these the positioning can be clearly examined. On the carve gybe you can note where the back foot is positioned, the extent of the kneebend and the rig position. What the pictures cannot show, however, is the timing and sequence used in a manoeuvre. In the carve gybe this is a good thing since a competent windsurfer will cut many corners of the original technique to make it smoother. For example, a good sailor gybing a short board changes his feet at the end of the turn; the novice attempting this would find it very difficult since at this stage you should change the feet before changing the rig. Advice from experts should therefore be approached with considerable caution, since although well intended it is often the interpretation of their own technique rather than that suitable for someone less experienced.

EXAGGERATING

If you have an idea of what is needed in a manoeuvre from a book or instructor, then exaggerating that particular aspect is often the best way to put it into practice. For instance, when coaching people in the carve gybe, rather than simply say 'Bend zee knees' which has little effect, it is better to ask them to try and get their knees to touch the water as they bank into the turn. Of course, this never actually happens but surprisingly people do seem to end up in the correct position. Exaggerating a physical movement often achieves the position that is being sought.

Mistakes

Every mistake is an opportunity to learn something. By being angry at our mistakes and mentally chastising ourselves we do not learn anything about why we fall. There is a danger that in getting angry with yourself, you try to *make* the learning happen rather than *allowing* it to happen.

Time is a great healer so rather than press on with a manoeuvre that is repeatedly failing, leave it for a while and come back to it later. By constantly making the same mistake there is the danger that you are reinforcing and learning how to make the error rather than correcting it.

It's All in the Mind

Learning a skill is in fact a fairly subconscious process. By practising the skill we show the subconscious what is involved and allow it to acquire the ability to master the skill. The more times we successfully complete a manoeuvre, the more opportunity we are giving the mind to reproduce the same movements. When practising or training, therefore, the greater the number of repetitions the better.

Whilst practising we should also insist on high standards, since once a technique is 'remembered' it is difficult to change. If you allow bad habits during practice, they will be difficult to lose later.

DAY-DREAMING

It might seem surprising, but day-dreaming can actually be useful. By rerunning successful events in the mind, such as that perfect smooth carve gybe you made, you are reinforcing your success. The more you relish the moment and remember exactly what it felt like and what movements were involved, the better. Mental repetition has been shown

Summary

1. Be honest about your present standard and evaluate realistic targets. This is called an 'end goal' and could be something like learning to carve gybe.
2. Always set yourself a time limit to achieve this by – but it must be flexible.
3. Break the manoeuvre down into key elements you can learn individually. These are the building blocks that will eventually form the structure for the whole skill, for example footsteering, speed, rig release.
4. If you want to improve your performance it is important that your body is ready for action. Warming up and stretching safely might not look particularly hip but as some of us now realise it gets more important as you age. Always allow the first fifteen minutes to 'settle' back into your sailing.
5. Mental rehearsal enables your body to go into automatic mode and is an invaluable tool – don't think, just do it! All too often, especially with intricate manoeuvres, your mind goes into overdrive and kills your natural instinct. Let your body go with the flow and remember that if you're not falling off you're not pushing the limits.
6. Use of video is an excellent tool for learning since it enables you to analyse yourself – actions speak louder than a thousand words. You must know someone who can help you here.

by research on basketball players to be as effective as going through the actions.

This approach is widely used in the competitive sphere, as David Hemery reports in *The Pursuit of Sporting Excellence* (Collins, 1986). Daley Thompson used to lie on his bed for much of the two days before a decathlon thinking his way through each event, mentally rehearsing the self-discipline needed when confronted with two failures at his first high jump or pole vault. Likewise John Newcombe would visualise the sequence from the dressing-room on to the court and the first few games to stem nervousness and condition his reactions in advance.

So, next time you prepare for the carve gybe think your way through it and imagine what it feels like to bear away, bending the knees and at the end flipping the rig.

1
Getting Started

EQUIPMENT

Types of Board

Board design has stabilised in recent years with most manufacturers producing similar designs – it is only the construction techniques and improved fittings that are still changing slightly.

The choices of board available are wide, which can confuse the uninitiated. It is therefore vital that you assess your sailing standard realistically and choose a board suitable for your needs and sailing location. Most retail outlets or windsurfing schools will be able to advise you if you are buying a board for the first time.

It is the volume of the board as well as the length that is most important for newcomers. More volume will provide greater stability. Obviously, a 75kg man will require more flotation that a 50kg woman.

Most boards these days are described under the loose and confusing term 'funboard'. This applies to any board with the following features: narrow tail, mast track, retractable daggerboard and footstraps.

The following is a description of some of the major board types. You will notice that the length of the board is used to help categorise them but there are deliberate omissions in the descriptions (such as 3.00–3.20m) where boards fall in between and display characteristics of two types.

LONGBOARD

This category covers a whole range of boards from roughly 3.45 to 3.80m in length. This is considered 'long'. The volume figures, ranging from about 180 to over 250 litres, will reveal how much weight the board can carry. All these boards have a centreboard and are extremely versatile, performing well in light and strong winds. Choose a board with a wider tail and soft sail option if you are a newcomer. It is also advisable to remove the footstraps as these tend to get in the way at first; as you improve they will help you control the board in stronger winds.

TRANSITIONAL (3.2–3.4m)

Boards of this length are mainly designed for use in Force 3+; they have a small daggerboard and are ideal for learning funboard manoeuvres since uphauling is still possible. They are ideally suited to ladies and children because of their light weight.

SHORT BOARDS (2.50–3.0m)

These come in various shapes and sizes suitable for first-timers, waves, slalom, speed or a combination of these uses. Water-starting skills need to be learned to get the best out of these boards and the smaller the board, the more important this is (*see* fig 70).

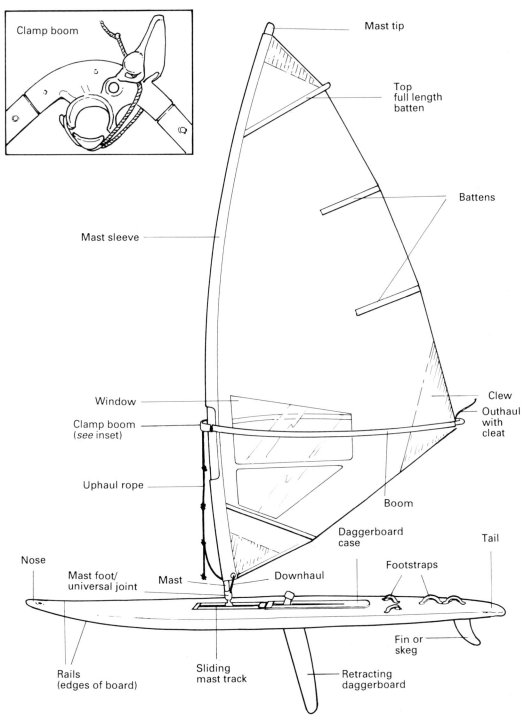

Clamp boom

Mast tip

Top
full length
batten

Battens

Mast sleeve

Window

Clamp boom
(*see* inset)

Uphaul rope

Clew

Outhaul
with
cleat

Boom

Daggerboard
case

Tail

Nose

Mast foot/
universal joint

Mast

Downhaul

Footstraps

Fin or
skeg

Rails
(edges of board)

Sliding
mast track

Retracting
daggerboard

Fig 2   The component parts of a windsurfer.

15

FIRST-TIME SHORT BOARD

Many people start off by using a 2.75m+ board for their first thrills. These shorter, highly responsive boards are characterised by high volume figures of 100–130 litres. The higher the figure the easier the board will be to uphaul and sail in marginal Force 3–4 conditions.

SLALOM BOARDS

There is great diversity here but most of these boards will have good speed and reasonable manoeuvrability. A real dedicated race machine will be too much of a handful for most folk.

WAVE BOARDS

These are designed to be turned hard on waves; speed is not particularly important since acceleration is provided by the wave face. They are characterised by their very low volume, and in the past have been referred to as 'sinkers' since they will not support a sailor's weight while stationary.

Types of Sail

There are many types of sail on the market today, each one offering attributes that favour specific types of sailing such as wave, slalom blasting and so on. The majority are made from mylar, sail cloth backed with a plastic-type film or monofilm, a thick transparent material. These modern sails are light, durable and extremely stable in comparison to their predecessors. An enthusiast will need a range of sail sizes to cover a range of wind conditions.

BEGINNERS SAIL
(Fig 3)
Most beginners learn using a soft sail, using sail sizes ranging from 4.5 to 5.5 sq m. The term 'soft' is used since the sail does not have full-length battens and hence is easy to uphaul, light, and offers excellent control in light winds. The next step would be to use a large rotational sail, which would give more power.

ROTATIONAL SAILS
(Fig 4)
These are also known as RAF sails (rotating asymmetrical foil) and have the front edge of the batten forced up close to the mast, providing more stability in stronger winds. They are popular on most beaches since they are easily used on long or short boards. A good sail of this type is ideal for learning the funboard skills described later on in this book. Initially newcomers will find the sail heavier but they will appreciate the additional power.

CAMBER INDUCED SAILS
(Fig 5)
Now if we are talking real power you'll want one of these; but at a price. They are often sold under a race or slalom-type label; the camber inducer is a plastic fork-like addition to the batten, which fits into the luff tube. The inducers create a deeper, more rigid foil shape, which encourages the air to flow smoothly around the mast. These heavier sails tend to have wide luff tubes, which consequently can fill with water, making water-starting difficult. A 'loose leach' is a characteristic of these sails that allows the tip of the sail to twist off in gusts, depowering the sail – this makes them more controllable.

WAVE SAILS
(Fig 6)
Wave sails normally have a dual batten system that combines the features of an

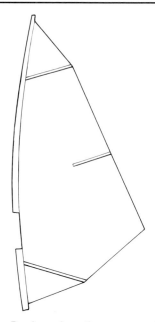

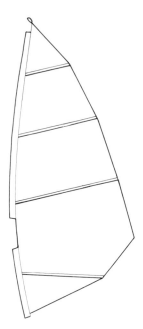

Fig 3   Beginner's sail: easy to uphaul, light and responsive in light winds. It is also cheap. Mainly used in windsurfing schools.

Fig 4   Rotational sail: a good all round sail which is stable and light.

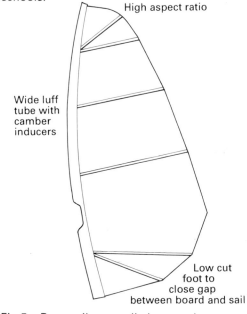

High aspect ratio

Wide luff tube with camber inducers

Low cut foot to close gap between board and sail

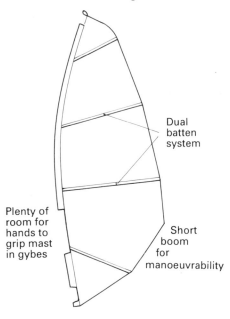

Dual batten system

Plenty of room for hands to grip mast in gybes

Short boom for manoeuvrability

Fig 5   Race sail: normally has camber inducers for extra power. Wide luff tube makes it heavy to uphaul/water start.

Fig 6   Wave sail: commonly used on short boards in open sea conditions.

RAF sail with a soft sail option. These sails aim to be easy to control in extreme conditions. They are designed for manoeuvrability not speed, as you are supposed to rip and slash when on the face of the wave. Features include a narrow luff tube, a high-cut foot and clew position, which makes water starting easy as well as extreme gybes – the idea here is to prevent the end of the boom catching in the waves. Tricks such as the duck gybe are also easier with this sail.

A NEWCOMER'S GUIDE TO BUYING EQUIPMENT

With so much equipment now available both new and second-hand, the choice can be quite daunting. Most shops stock a variety of boards at differing prices. It is worth while looking through the current magazines so that you become familiar with brand names and what may be available to you. Shop around, as prices vary considerably. Here is some practical advice to help you choose correctly.

Vital Considerations

BUY A BIG BOARD

The best measure of overall size is the volume of a board, so by big I mean over 200 litres of volume. Sometimes the volume quoted by the manufacturer is wrong by as much as 25 per cent, so press the salesman to confirm that the volume of the board is at least 200 litres. The length of the board should be greater than 3.60m unless the user is a slight lady or a child, in which case the length and volume can be less than the figures quoted above.

The perfect board needs to have enough volume to make it a stable platform for you to learn on, which in turn allows you to learn quickly and easily.

LARGE FULLY RETRACTING DAGGERBOARD

Make sure that the board you buy has a large daggerboard which retracts fully into the hull. The daggerboard should always be down while learning as it provides stability as well as lateral resistance (which keeps you tracking in a straight line). As you improve and start to sail in stronger winds, you will want to retract the daggerboard; this prevents the board from railing and helps with control in stronger winds. By altering the daggerboard position you can markedly change the board's characteristics.

AN EASY-TO-HANDLE RIG

If you have completed an RYA 'Learn to Windsurf' course, you will have learnt on a soft sail. Assuming you have mastered the basics, you could, like most people, purchase a beginner's package complete with rotational sail. These feel slightly heavier to start with and have more power but you will soon appreciate this as you improve. Ideally you want two sails: one should be around 5.7 sq m and the other one, for use in stronger winds, should be around 4.5 sq m. Boom length is a vital consideration; too long a boom makes uphauling difficult, while too short a boom affects steering ability in light winds.

Unless you want to make things difficult for yourself *don't buy a board which fails to satisfy all three of the above requirements*.

Secondary Considerations

FOOTSTRAPS

These are only used when you can sail the board competently in a Force 4. On most boards the footstraps can be fitted when you improve so on no account should they be on the board when you are learning as they can get in your way as you step around the board.

MAST TRACK

Nearly all boards today have a sliding mast track which moves the mastfoot. To start with, place it in the middle and don't move it until you have reached RYA Level 3. A sliding mastfoot enables you to change the board's sailing characteristics as follows: moving it forward increases the lateral resistance for upwind work, while moving it back reduces the wetted surface area for planning manoeuvres.

MODERN SHAPE

What you should avoid is a board with a very wide square tail. The tail should resemble something like a rounded surf-board tail. Another factor here is the underwater shape which, like footstraps, will become more important as you improve. A concave underwater shape will give superior performance when you progress to an intermediate level. The modern tail and underwater shapes will enable you to make progress in stronger wind and sail far quicker than if you use a wide square-tailed board with a flat bottom. A modern shape is faster and enables you to steer the board with your feet at high speeds.

CLOTHING

Unless you live in a warm climate a wet suit is essential. A wet suit keeps you warm by trapping a thin layer of warm water between the skin and neoprene, which provides added insulation. Without one, your time on the water will be greatly reduced. It must be tight fitting and allow reasonable freedom of movement. One-piece steamers are the best option.

A buoyancy aid is also a good idea and may be useful later on when learning to water start. Modern buoyancy aids are considerably less bulky than their predecessors.

Although to start with you can use ordinary sports shoes, in the long term it is worth while investing in some purpose-designed windsurfing footwear. Good windsurfing boots or shoes have soft rubber soles so your grip will be far better, and the materials used in them mean that they can withstand use in water much better than running shoes. They also keep your feet warm.

Longer Term Considerations

TRANSPORTATION

One of the attractions of windsurfing is that the equipment can be transported so easily. All you need is a sturdy roof-rack that attaches to the guttering of the car, and, rather than relying on your knot-tying ability, you can buy special straps that make securing the board, mast and boom far easier.

INSURANCE

Last but not least it is a good idea to take out insurance, preferably with comprehensive and at least third party cover. The incidence of board theft is thankfully low but it does happen. However, there is always the remote possibility that you might run down and injure someone in the water, which could cost you as much as £100,000! Third party insurance will cover you against this unlikely possibility and in Britain costs little more than £10. There are specialist brokers who deal in this type of insurance whose addresses you can normally find through your local shop or in windsurfing magazines.

Buying Second Hand

Buying a second-hand board is rather like the second-hand car or computer market in that there are plenty of bargains but unless you are careful you can be ripped off. Older boards tend to have a fixed mastfoot and a daggerboard that doesn't fully retract, making it difficult to improve. The rig can be very unstable, which will hinder your development. You can still learn on these older boards and at as little as £150 they can be a real bargain. Some people learn on a cheaper second-hand board and once they are sure they want to pursue the sport they buy a modern board on which to progress. These older boards still sail perfectly well in lighter winds and it is only when you start improving to stronger wind conditions that the difference becomes apparent.

Like the car market you can either buy a second-hand board from a shop or privately. A shop will prove a little more expensive but may be able to offer some kind of a guarantee. A shop should also be able to demonstrate the availability of spare parts for the board you have selected.

Buying privately you can pick up some excellent equipment, but it is best to obtain some independent advice from someone who knows what they are talking about. The board should be checked for damage, especially around the nose and rails, and it is also worth bearing in

mind its weight since boards become heavier with age. The rig will also need a thorough check for signs of wear and tear.

WHERE TO LEARN

To learn the basics of the sport it is best to go to one of the numerous windsurfing schools around the country. There is an excellent course of standardised tuition which has been organised in the UK by the Royal Yachting Association (RYA). The cost is very reasonable, starting at around £30, and the course can be completed in a day, either during the week or over a weekend, in safe, flat water conditions.

Some people ask a friend to show them the ropes or, worse still, they teach themselves. We all know the limitations of a friend teaching you to drive – the finer points are never brought out unless the friend is himself an instructor. Sometimes it is not very safe either.

Most windsurfing schools are run by shops and the format consists of dry land practice on a simulator followed by sessions on the water, with wetsuits, buoyancy aids and safety boat provided. By the end of the course you will be able to sail the board in light winds, in any direction and get home again.

Learning Abroad

A large number of people sample windsurfing whilst on holiday and unfortunately do so under difficult conditions: crowded swimming beaches, choppy conditions, poor equipment and indifferent instruction.

If this applies to you, next time try and find a genuine windsurfing school away from the crowded beaches with qualified English-speaking instructors. The RYA has a list of schools it recognises as fulfilling its requirements and it may be worth contacting them. Alternatively, you could take a holiday specifically with the aim of windsurfing, as these carefully chosen centres are often in pleasant holiday surroundings.

BASIC TECHNIQUE

Since a book by itself cannot teach you to windsurf from scratch, this beginner's section is a guide to be referred to. It is not a 'how to do it' text but rather one that is best read in conjunction with an RYA Level 1 course.

Assembling and Carrying the Equipment

Most boards use very similar methods for assembly and come with a full set of instructions. It is usually fairly easy to work out any variations from the norm.

The rig, which is the collective name for the sail, mast and boom, should be put together in the following manner:

1. The mast is slid into the sleeve of the sail and the mastfoot/universal joint is pushed into the bottom of the mast.
2. The downhaul line is tied and lightly tensioned to the bottom of the sail. There is often a pulley and cleat provided for this purpose, but on some older boards where it is not present you will have to improvise by making a loop in the bottom of the line.
3. The next stage is to attach the boom to the mast. You should set it so that it is level with your shoulders; to check this raise the mast beside you and mark the point. Modern booms use a clamp system which is quick and easy to adjust. If you have a boom that uses the tie-on method,

Fig 7   Attaching the boom. Modern booms use a clamp system which is quick and easy to adjust (*see also* fig 2). Older rope systems can easily be changed to clamp by buying a new boom front end.

CARRYING YOUR EQUIPMENT

Fig 8 *(Above)* Carry the board using one hand on the daggerboard and the other in the mast track.

Fig 9a *(Above right)* When carrying the sail use one hand on the boom and the other on the mast. Ensure that the boom is always pointing into wind.

Fig 9b *(Right)* Let the wind do the work! Flying the mast at right angles to the wind makes this overhead method easy.

attach it when the boom is parallel to the mast to ensure a tight connection.

4. Tension the outhaul. Again, pulleys and cleats are provided to make this easier. You should make full use of them since the sail should be tight.

5. If the sail is fully battened, insert each batten and tension it using the webbing strap and buckle until the creases along the batten pocket disappear. They should not need much adjusting since most sails of this type are rolled during storage.

6. Having done all this, final adjustments can be made to the downhaul and outhaul to ensure that the sail has a good aerofoil shape. The common mistake is that people are afraid to pull too hard for fear of breaking something. The result is a baggy shape which is difficult to use. Pull tighter than you think necessary, aiming to produce a smooth shape without any creases. If in doubt ask for advice.

The board needs little preparation since once the skeg is attached only the daggerboard has to be slid into its case. On no account should footstraps be fitted at the novice stage, as they will only get in your way.

Dropping boards and sails through not carrying them correctly can be very expensive, so it is worth learning the correct method (Figs 8 and 9). The easiest way to carry the board is with one hand in the daggerboard and the other on the mast track. The board should balance well in this position.

When preparing to sail the board should be left by the edge of the water and the rig should be put in the water first. If the board is left unattended in the water it can drift away very quickly as the wind and waves catch it, whereas the rig only drifts very slowly.

Finally, the rig can be attached to the board. Again, each manufacturer uses a slightly different system, but they nearly all have a mechanism which controls how easily the mastfoot releases from the board. This should be set so that it only comes out under considerable pressure.

Raising the Rig

Uphauling is simple as long as you use the correct technique! Keeping your feet on the centreline, with your knees bent and your back straight, lean with straight

Fig 10   Remember technique is important here. Note that the feet are over the centre line with knees bent. Lean back without jerking and let your body weight and not your back pull the sail clear. See how the arms are relatively straight as you are trying to raise the mast tip from the water.

23

arms against the pull. As the sail begins to emerge work hand over hand up the rope.

Do not pull the sail out of the water so quickly that when the sail flies clear you fall backwards into the water. When the sail and boom are clear of the water, transfer your hands to the mast, placing them below the boom. Remember to keep an imaginary 'V' shape between your body and the mast.

Turning Practice

A common complaint from people who have not been taught properly is often: 'I could get the sail up all right and sail a little, but I couldn't turn round and come back.' Learning how to turn is obviously an important skill that should be mastered before you sail away. Your instructor will insist that you can do this before progressing any further.

Once the rig is raised and your hands are on the mast you can turn the board by inclining the rig to either end of the board. To stop the board turning, just like a car's steering-wheel, you return the rig to a

Turning Round and Steering
1. To get back to where you came from put your hands back on to the mast in the secure position and lean the rig to the front or back of the board to turn it. Take small steps around the mast until you find yourself heading back in the right direction.
2. To steer whilst sailing use your hands on the boom to angle the mast towards the front or back of the board. This will turn it into and away from the wind respectively.

neutral middle position. Whilst doing this you must keep the end of the boom out of the water since if it 'catches', the wind will fill the sail and control will be lost.

To turn the board round through 180 degrees keep leaning the sail towards one end of the board and take small shuffling steps around the mast as the board turns under you. Try to avoid looking down at your feet as you do this. When you have turned completely, stop the board turning by bringing the rig back to the middle.

When turning completely it is always preferable to turn by leaning the sail over the *back* of the board (a tack) since this will turn the board into wind and make it easier to return from where you set out. Although leaning the sail over the front of the board (a gybe) is easier, it often makes getting back more difficult since you have to sail further into wind.

Using these newly acquired turning skills the board can be lined up into the *secure position* from which you can start sailing. This position is reached when the board faces directly across the wind, the sail making a right angle with the board. Once you have mastered finding and maintaining this position you are ready to sail.

Setting Off
(Figs 11 to 14)

Remember that before you start to sail the board must be in the secure position.

GRIP ON THE BOOM

Use whatever grip feels comfortable, overhand grip (palms down) or underhand grip (palms up) – concentrate on keeping your hands shoulder-width apart.

Fig 11   The secure position. The board is facing across the wind, the sail is at right angles to the board. Keep your feet on the centreline and grasp the mast with straight arms. Leave the rope alone: it's only there for uphauling.

FEET

The foot placement is very important as it encourages the rest of the body to take up a good position. The front foot faces forwards; this should help the upper body to rotate facing the front. The back foot is placed across the board on the centreline at a comfortable distance behind the front foot.

RIG POSITION

The next step is crucial because if the rig is not pulled across in front of the body all sorts of problems will arise. Remember: pull the rig across to a balanced position using the front hand on the mast. A good guide is that the front of the board should be visible through the sail window.

SHEETING IN

Applying the power to the sail is the next stage and a useful analogy here is that of closing a door. Imagine the front hand on the mast is holding the hinge and the

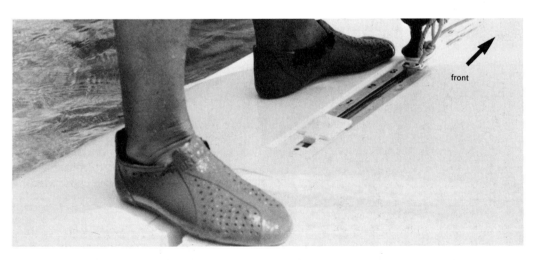

Fig 12   Get that front foot back *behind* the mastfoot. The back foot is placed across the middle of the board about shoulder width behind the front foot. You'll place more weight on this foot if the wind increases.

25

pull rig well across
before sheeting in

WIND

Fig 13   Just before setting off: the rig is pulled across the body towards the wind until it feels balanced. If you fail to pull the rig across in this manner you will be making it very difficult for yourself.

Fig 14   A little imagination is needed here. Imagine the hand on the boom is pulling the door closed, using the hand on the mast as the hinge. By closing the door like this (sheeting in), you put power into the sail and start moving.

other (back) hand is placed on the boom level with the shoulder – as the imaginary door is closed, the power comes on. The more you sheet in, the greater the power.

LEAN, DON'T PULL

Once the power is applied, the sail (rather unsportingly) tries to pull you over. Rather than tensing up and pulling with all your arm strength, simply use your weight to do the work for you by leaning on your arms with a straight back. Most of your weight should be on the back foot.

Leaning rather than pulling is a recur-

rent theme in windsurfing which, once mastered, leads to rapid progress.

Balancing

Keeping your weight on the centreline is a fairly obvious tip, but you can also stay upright by varying the power in the sail. So, if you are being pulled over, rather than letting go of the boom completely and having to raise the rig again, you can save a lot of time and energy by letting out the back hand until you have regained control. The opposite applies if you feel

If You Fall off . . .
1. To get back onto the board swim towards the middle of the board and place both hands on the centre line behind the mast.
2. Kick hard with your feet and push with your hands so you can get one, or preferably both, knees on to the board.
3. If you find this difficult, use the mast to help you. This will be in the water beside the board and can be used to help you push up with one hand on the mast and one on the centre line of the board.

yourself falling in backwards – pull in the back hand to give yourself more power.

Start to anticipate gusts and lulls in the wind.

Steering

This is done by angling the rig forwards or backwards. Most problems arise when inclining the rig to the front to turn the board away from the wind; if you commit too much weight forwards there is a risk of being pulled over. Try to transfer the weight on to your back foot and maintain a crouched position which keeps your centre of gravity lower. Also, as the theory section shows, sheeting in will help.

The Emergency Stop
Where there is the danger of colliding with or hitting something, rather than abandoning ship and letting the board glide unaided on to the 'target', it is far better to fall in, bringing the rig with you, which will stop it instantly.

Getting Back
(Figs 15 and 16)

From the sailing position, transfer your hands from the boom to the mast (back hand first), so you are in the secure position again. Simply turn the board through 180 degrees as explained earlier.

SELF HELP

If you cannot get back to shore use a self rescue technique. Two of the most useful methods are shown in Figs 15 and 16 *(overleaf)*.

An important safety rule is never to leave your board unless it is to get into a safety boat, since your board will make it easier for rescuers to see you and will keep you afloat.

WINDSURFING THEORY

At first sight this might all look very technical, but it is really fairly simple, and an understanding of the theory of how a board works will help you to progress beyond a beginner's level.

The Sail
(Figs 17 and 18)

Let's start with the sail. This is a curved surface in a moving airflow which simply bends the wind, causing a pressure difference between the windward and leeward sides of the sail. Where there is a pressure difference, air will attempt to move from high to low pressure. For example, in a bicycle tyre the high pressure air inside tries to force its way out creating enough force on the rubber to support a human. On our sail the pressure difference causes a driving force

27

GETTING BACK

Fig 15   If you cannot get back and the wind is very light, by carefully balancing the rig on the back of the board you can lie down on the front and paddle back.

Fig 15b   Yes, it does look a bit odd but it can get you home in emergencies.

Fig 16   Another method of getting back is to take the battens out and roll the sail up towards the mast. Then, by placing it on the board again, you can lie down and paddle home. These methods are difficult in stronger winds.

which acts roughly at right angles to the sail at its centre of effort (Fig 17).

If we transfer this sail to a board which is restrained by its daggerboard from moving sideways, we can look more closely at the driving force (Fig 18). When sailing across the wind (reaching) the driving force D is acting in almost exactly the required direction, giving the board plenty of forward force F, but only a small amount of sideways force S, which the daggerboard can easily resist. Sailing close to the wind (beating), the greatest force is sideways with only a small forward force. Here the daggerboard is straining to stop the board slipping sideways. Sailing with the wind behind the sail (running) simply pulls the board

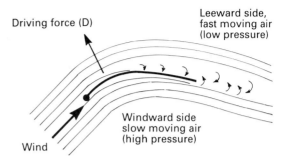

Fig 17   Producing the driving force.

along and, in this case, although the daggerboard has no sideways forces to resist, it can help by giving the board stability.

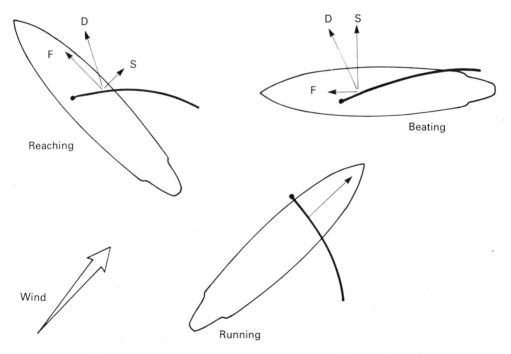

Fig 18   On the reach the forwards force F is large, whilst the sideways force S is small. When beating it is the sideways force that is large with the daggerboard fully down to resist it. When sailing with the wind on the run, the driving force D acts forwards.

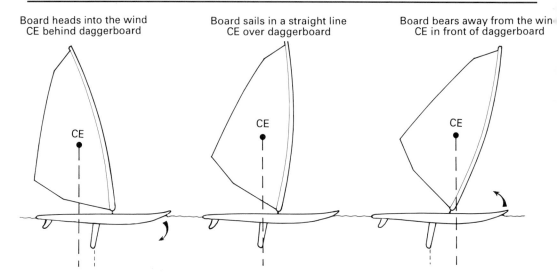

Board heads into the wind
CE behind daggerboard

Board sails in a straight line
CE over daggerboard

Board bears away from the wind
CE in front of daggerboard

CE

CE

CE

Fig 19   Steering by inclining the rig forwards or backwards.

Steering

BY MOVING THE RIG
(Fig 19)

As we said earlier, the driving force acts through an imaginary centre of effort (CE) on the sail. Similarly, the sideways resistance of the board, which is largely controlled by the daggerboard, acts through the imaginary centre of lateral resistance (CLR). When steering by moving the rig forwards or backwards we are moving the CE either side of the daggerboard, which is the fulcrum about which the board turns. When sailing in a straight line the CE will be almost directly over the CLR (the daggerboard).

WITHOUT MOVING THE RIG
(Fig 20)

This is often an unintentional form of steering which happens when the sail is not at the correct angle to the wind – the section of the sail next to the mast does not fill with wind and the driving force acts from a couple of feet further back. The CE

has moved behind the CLR and the board steers into wind. This is commonly known as luffing.

This situation commonly arises in stronger winds when the inexperienced sailor lacks the technique to sheet in fully, so he edges along partly 'closing the door', and as a result slowly turns into wind. Frantic attempts to sail a straight

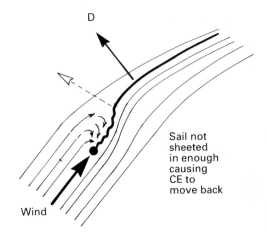

D

Sail not sheeted in enough causing CE to move back

Wind

Fig 20   Steering without moving the rig.

course by inclining the rig forwards usually fail as the CE is so far back. Unfortunately the effect is cumulative, since once the board starts turning into the wind it is even harder to sheet in the sail fully. The solution is to use a smaller sail until your technique improves.

STEERING DIFFICULTIES

It should now be clear why the daggerboard must be fully down, as not only does it provide stability but also the pivot point about which the board turns.

Fig 21   Steering on a run. By pushing the sail over to the right-hand side of the board the CE is also moved, causing the board to steer to the left. Notice that on a run the feet are placed across the board and the body faces the front.

Steering difficulties often arise with the use of small short boom sails and especially childrens' rigs on full size boards. In these cases the arc of movement of the rig is not great enough to get the CE sufficiently behind the CLR and so the board becomes unresponsive. A solution to this can be to cut down the skeg, as this provides the resistance at the back of the board.

Summary Tips

Getting the sail up (uphauling)
• Make sure the daggerboard is fully down and the wind is on your back.
• Keep feet on the centre line.
• Knees bent, back straight – apply a constant pull, don't jerk.
• Transfer hands to mast as soon as sail is clear of the water.

Setting Sail
• Before you begin, choose a goal point that is across the wind and form a mental picture of what is upwind/downwind.
• Always begin from the secure position.
• Move your feet back behind the mastfoot.
• Ensure that you pull the rig across your body before you apply the power.
• Keep the weight on your back foot and look towards your goal point.

Turning
• Return to the secure position.
• Always incline the rig over the back of the board. This keeps you from straying too far downwind.
• Keep arms straight and take small shuffling steps around mast.
• Take your time, don't rush – the board will turn in a wide arc.

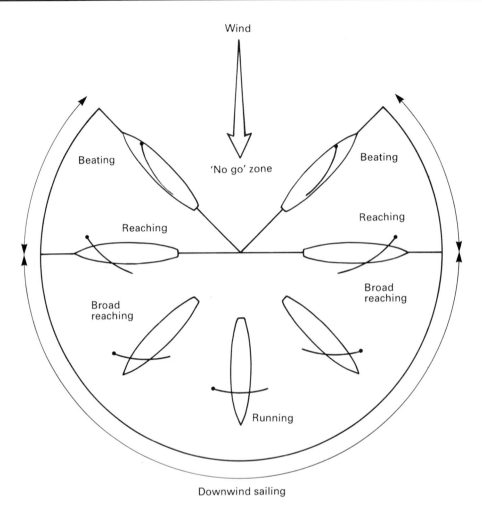

Fig 22   Points of sailing and the 'no go' zone.

The 'No Go' Zone
(Fig 22)

Sailing craft cannot sail directly into the wind but only at an angle of 45 degrees to it. If the board is sailed too close to the wind, the so called 'no go' zone is entered within which the board will stop or even blow backwards. Progress upwind can only be made by completing a series of zigzags, the turns at first being executed by the 180 degree turn method and later, with more experience, by tacking – steering the board through the turn.

2
Improving Techniques

EXERCISES AND GAMES

It is often said that children can pick up and learn things much quicker than adults. This is probably the case since children do things the way that feels natural for them without worrying unduly how it is meant to be done. They use instinct and spontaneity and when they practise something, they do so for the enjoyment it produces and thus it becomes more of a game than a practice.

On windsurfers children are particularly quick learners since they spend much of their time messing about on boards, and in the process find out how to handle their boards and rigs in a number of unorthodox positions. In showing off their agility in a Force 2 they learn what not to do to remain upright in a Force 5. Children at play do things that inhibited adults would never do. They learn all the wrong ways of doing things and so learn what to avoid.

How to Play

This section, then, like child's play, suggests a number of exercises and games which will help to develop an awareness of how the board behaves. They are all a type of experimentation, which was outlined as being an important part of learning in the opening chapter.

Every drill or game has a purpose: to learn. There are often other purposes too – some are obvious, others less so. Sometimes the purpose will be described but often it won't, since you may try to anticipate the result.

You need to select flat water conditions with no more than a Force 3 otherwise you will be concentrating too hard on staying upright rather than thinking about the exercises.

I have grouped exercises using similar skills into four sets, which are themselves closely related: they are posture, balance, control and pairs.

Posture

LOOKING AROUND YOU
Whilst sailing along with a comfortable posture, pick out all the details of the water and land around you. Don't just limit this to everything in front of you, but look *all* around you, even behind you and on the other side of the sail. Notice what shades of colour there are on the water and look at your wake as it shoots from under the board. How many other boards are there on the water? Look at the surrounding skyline and pick out things that catch the eye – the flashy Porsche, that dark cloud looming or an ugly building that sticks out like a sore thumb.

SAILING STIFFLY
As you are sailing along, tense up and sail

33

stiffly with your hands clutching the boom with a vice-like grip, with arms locked solid and body rigid. Hold it for a few seconds, maybe five, then release it. Remember the posture you adopted when you first learned? Try that – hands wide apart and crouched a bit like a gorilla, pulling hard with the arms on the boom. Each time you relax, revert back to your own stance and feel the benefit of the comparison.

ROTATING

Try rotating your hips in all the different directions possible, facing both forwards and backwards. Now do the same with your shoulders and experiment with which of the positions feels most comfortable.

Balance

Deep inside our ears is the mechanism for keeping us balanced. When our mechanism is level (i.e. when the head is level) balance is natural. When our mechanism is itself not level, any corrections to the body have a built-in bias which has to be overcome before balance is regained.

TRY THIS

Stand on one leg in front of a mirror and watch your eyes in the mirror. Now tilt your head slightly. Do you notice a compensating reaction in your foot?

Whilst windsurfing, by keeping the head level you are giving the body the best chance of keeping its balance beneath you. Now you know this, don't start applying it rigorously as a rule which will inhibit your sailing, merely let the body work it out for itself by noticing the levelness of the horizon.

WINDSURFING BLIND

Pick an open, clear area of water and close your eyes for short intervals, gradually making them longer at each attempt. As you will find, we only need our eyes to tell us where to go since windsurfing is done completely by feel. It is a good indication that once a skill is learned, reproducing it is purely instinctive.

ARMS AND HANDS

Try feeling the different pressures in each arm as you sail along. Aim to try and make the pressure equal in each arm by moving the hands up or down the boom. Experiment with moving the hands closer together or further apart, again noticing how the pressures change. As you move both hands forwards or backwards which arm takes more weight?

Try and place one hand in a balanced enough position to take the strain of the whole rig, letting go with the other one.

FEET

Similarly to the hands, feel the way the weight is distributed over both feet. By moving the feet around the board try and get your wake to be as quiet as possible and watch how it differs as you move your weight around.

You can not only experiment with different feet positions and weighting but also with the angle at which the feet are placed across the board. There are numerous variations possible, so experiment with different feet angles and see which one suits your style best. The way you angle your feet determines the posture of the lower body.

Gradually take all the weight off one foot but leave it on the board as a back-up. When you are ready, take it off the board and waggle it about.

Fig 23   One hand. Notice the position of the hand on the boom and also how straight the arm is.

Fig 24   Crouching. Note the positioning of the feet on the centreline. How else, besides using her leg muscles, might she be able to help herself to stand up?

If you are feeling really confident, you can try one foot and one hand together.

Control

Freestyle is an excellent way of developing control over the board. The exercises that follow are based on some of the easier freestyle manoeuvres, but the great thing about freestyle is that you can invent your own tricks.

OVERSHEETING

By deliberately pulling in the sail too tight over the back of the board you can try sailing sideways or even backwards. This is also a good method of making someone else fall in without even touching them, since if you sail directly upwind of someone and then oversheet the sail, you create such a disturbed and confused wind that it becomes very difficult to sail in.

SAILING INSIDE THE BOOM

By crouching down, you can rise up inside the boom and rest your back on it.

SITTING DOWN

This is a particularly good practice for developing the idea of transferring your

35

body weight through the mast foot. At first you will only be able to crouch down on the board, but as you get used to pulling down on the booms to pull yourself up again, you will be able to get lower. Some people even lie on the board.

BACKWARDS

Pretend you are a beginner who has inadvertently forgotten which end of the board is forwards and set sail going backwards. See how far you can sail like this.

SAILING ON THE WRONG SIDE

Do a tack but don't walk around the front of the board. To get the power back on again you will now have to push against the sail as you sail on the wrong side. This is a unique feeling as instead of your arms pulling on the boom, you are looking from the other side of the sail and pushing.

TAIL SINK
(Fig 25)

As the name implies, you walk towards the back of the board, thereby sinking the tail. This can only be done when sailing directly with the wind on a run. It is very good practice, since you will find that by using your weight, which is so far back, you can steer the board downwind.

If you feel adventurous, try sailing backwards and then doing a *nose* sink.

WIND

Fig 25 Tail sink. A very good exercise to practise using the weight to steer. You can control the amount of 'sink' by either pulling up, as I am doing here, or pushing down on the boom.

Pairs

FOLLOWING
Sailing closely with someone is a very good way of practising. Try following them as closely as possible, almost touching their tail. This will need very good control.

TAG
This close following can easily turn into a competitive game of tag. You can also play this with a number of boards, but it is best to avoid tagging each other by board contact, which becomes rather dangerous if people start ramming each other.

If you set an area outside which you cannot sail then tag one another by doing a tack or gybe around them, it can turn into a very good game where you can build up your own tactics. In fact, I have always thought it would make a great spectacle for television if performed in surf with three contestants confined to a small area, all trying to knock each other off their boards. The audience would love the thrills and spills with the added spice of danger.

HUMAN VIDEO
By sailing along behind someone you can act as a human video and when your partner has finished his run you can mimic what he was doing. This often leads to each sailor offering the other useful and constructive criticism about his windsurfing. If you can find a partner of roughly the same level, this is an excellent way of practising.

FASTER TURNING

As you progress you will want to turn quicker and in a smaller radius. Turning into wind is called tacking, turning away from the wind gybing. The key to faster tacking is speed around the mastfoot and a low body position, which keeps you stable and stops you from being pulled forwards.

The Quick Tack
(Figs 26 to 28)

Key Points
Enter the tack with speed; keep low; weight on the back foot; don't swap sides until the board is past head to wind; throw the rig forward on the new tack;
Wind Force 1 to 6
Daggerboard Down

THE RIG
To get the maximum effect from the CE the rig has to be inclined as far back as possible. The best way to achieve this is to place the front hand on the mast below the boom as you lean the rig back. Try and make the end of the boom skim the water. In stronger winds, as the theory section explains, you can head up by deliberately sheeting out.

BODY POSITION
The most important aspect of this is to place all your weight on your back foot as you turn. The weighted back foot should also slightly depress the leeward rail. In the process of heading up, place your front foot by the mastfoot in anticipation of the rush to get round to the new tack.

THE QUICK TACK

Fig 26 Approach the tack with speed as this helps momentum throughout. The daggerboard should be down and mast track towards the front. From a close-hauled position, the front hand is transferred to the mast and the front foot goes around the front of the mastfoot. As the rig is inclined back and down on to the footstraps, nearly all the weight is on the back foot. Sheet in hard and keep low.

Fig 27 Notice how the sail has been sheeted in so much that the sail touches the shin. From this position you need to swap sides on the board in as few steps as possible. At the right moment your weight is transferred to your front foot and at the same time the rig drawn more upright. Remember the importance of staying in a low crouched position and keeping the feet close to the centreline.

THE TRANSFER

Timing is critical here. Steer the board through the eye of the wind until the sail brushes on your back leg, before trans- ferring both back hand and foot up to the mast. The quicker you can get around the mast the better, some people even jump, but the main point is that both hands

Fig 28a   Our sailor is now on the new tack and the most noticeable feature is that he is sheeting in the sail almost immediately he gets around the mast. The problem is that when applying the power in this position you also have to lean the sail forwards to encourage the board to complete the turn; this is an unstable position that requires a lot of weight on the back foot. Note also that there is nothing wrong with sheeting in with one hand still on the mast.

Fig 28b   As the board picks up speed the normal sailing position can be adopted though you can see how a wide, low body position is still providing stability.

should hold the mast and not the uphaul rope. Once on the new side, the rig should be thrown well forwards to complete the turn on to the new tack.

EXERCISE
Experiment with varying positions and different amounts of weight on the back foot when you head into the wind.

The Flare Gybe
(Figs 29 to 33)

The flare gybe uses a combination of daggerboard-down footsteering and marked rig angulation to increase the speed of the gybe and control the board's turning arc. For this manoeuvre the daggerboard is down and the turn shouldn't be confused with the carve gybe, which is performed at planing speed with the daggerboard retracted.

Key Points
Angle the rig forwards and across the board; keep low; depress windward rail; kill turn by moving forwards; use an efficient rig change.
Wind Force 1 to 4
Centreboard Slightly swept back

INITIATING THE TURN
Don't enter the turn with too much speed; you may need to slow down. The rig

WIND

WIND

THE FLARE GYBE

Fig 29 The board is steered away from the wind by initially inclining the rig forwards and then leaning it over the windward side of the board. Once the board has started to turn, move back on the board and apply weight to the windward rail, as Peter Hart is doing here.

Fig 30 With the weight well back on the board and still on the windward (left) edge, the board will continue to turn swiftly. The rig is also used to encourage the turn by using the same steering technique as on a run.

Fig 31 The board is now well through the turn, and to stop it turning too far take the weight off the edge and move forwards. Notice how with this change in weight distribution the nose is closer to the water, and the rails next to the mastfoot are engaging the water which slows the turn.

Fig 32 With the weight well forward again, the nose is in the water offering far more resistance to turning than when it was in the air. It is now time for the all-important rig change, so the back hand is released from the boom . . .

This hand releases and grasps the mast

Fig 33 . . . and is placed on the mast below the boom. The rig will swing over the front of the board and try to pull you over. Keep low and vigorously throw the rig across the board (to the right) before attempting to sheet in.

Pull mast vigorously into wind before sheeting in

should initially be inclined forwards and then drawn to the side of the board as it approaches the broad reaching position. The front foot should be on the windward edge and well weighted.

THE TURN

The rig is still inclined over the side of the board; in lighter winds it may be necessary to move your hands well down the boom to make this effective. The turn can be speeded up if you take a step back on the board and depress the windward rail. Once the board has turned you will have to move forwards quickly to kill the turn before it goes too far.

FLIPPING THE RIG

From the clew first position release your back hand and place it on the mast below the boom. As soon as it is firmly on the boom release your other hand. The mast hand then vigorously throws the rig across the body ready for the new back hand to sheet in. It is especially important to keep low when sheeting in.

EXERCISE

A useful exercise to practise the rig steering combined with weight on the rails is to see how long you can maintain the freestyle trick of tail sinking. Notice how sensitive the board is to weight movements the further back you step.

THE DAGGERBOARD AND WEIGHT DISTRIBUTION

The Daggerboard
(Fig 34)

A great deal of confusion surrounds the use of the daggerboard. It has two uses:

1. It provides the main resistance to the sideways forces of the sail.
2. It gives the board stability at low speeds.

Thus, in lighter winds, it should be kept *down* on all points of sailing.

However, when the speed of the board increases to near planing speed in stronger winds, problems start arising which can ultimately lead to a *capsize fall.* As the name suggests, the board literally flips over on its side and you usually tumble off when sailing fast on a reach.

A capsize fall is caused by the forces acting on the daggerboard at high speeds *(see* Fig 34). In resisting the sideways forces the daggerboard starts to behave like a sail and a force is set up between the high and low pressure sides of the foil (F_1). Not only does this force encourage the board to capsize, but the weight of the sailor carried on the boom is transmitted through the mastfoot (M). These combined forces cause the board to capsize.

There are two solutions. Firstly, the weight transmitted through the sailor's feet can be used to counter the capsize by placing them on the rail (W_2). Secondly, if the daggerboard is raised the force (F_2) will not be so effective in turning the board over.

So, in stronger winds on a reach or run the daggerboard is either partially or completely raised, and all the sideways resistance is left to the skeg and rails. Upwind, however, the daggerboard is still kept in the down position, though in extreme conditions it needs to be moved back a few centimetres.

Remember: if the daggerboard is swept back it also moves the CE back, thus making bearing away easier but heading up more difficult.

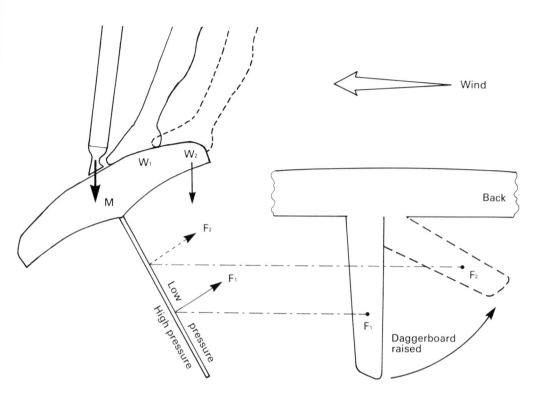

Fig 34 The capsize fall.

Weight Distribution
(Figs 35 and 36)

This was touched upon when discussing the flare gybe. By placing your weight on either side of the board it is possible to footsteer it, as Fig 35 shows. This *only* applies when the daggerboard is *down*. Basically, by weighting the left rail the board turns to the right and vice versa. This is why when you tack it is important to weight the leeward edge as you turn. The further back you apply the weight, the greater the effect. The tail sink exercise described earlier is an excellent way of practising this.

To increase the board's speed and performance it needs to be sailed flat. Where

Fig 35 Steering using weight.

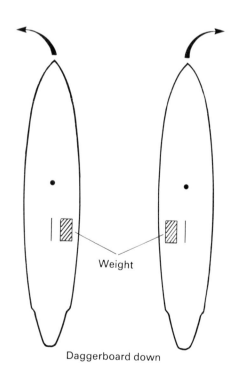

43

upwind   as wind increases move feet on to rail
to counter capsize fall

Fig 36a   Upwind foot positioning. Notice how the feet are relatively square across the board just behind the daggerboard. As the wind increases they move back towards the windward rail to counter the railing effect. Turn to fig 98 to see how far Penny Way has got her feet across the board in a Force 4.

reaching   as wind increases move back, keeping board level

Fig 36b   Reaching. The feet are moved further back as the wind increases. Notice how as you progress the feet point across the board compared to the learning position of fig 12. Keep the board level.

you place your feet will have an effect on this. Far too many people sink the back of the board in attempting to get their feet in the footstraps. All this does is kill the speed, which in turn will make them spin into wind. Remember your weight is distributed through your feet *and* through the mastfoot. By moving the mastfoot forwards or back you can trim the board efficiently. A good way of checking your trim is to look behind you and try to maintain a small and quiet wake.

NEW HORIZONS

Most sailors soon tire of sailing in the same place all the time and look for new places to sail which will give them variety and a challenge. The unknown adds spice to the adventure, whether it is a relative newcomer's first trip to windsurf on the sea, or a move to a place that provides more of a challenge with better waves for an aspiring expert. Either way, this section looks at some of the things you should think about when arriving at a new location.

Choosing Where to Go

Many people rely on personal recommendations as to where to head for. These can be fairly reliable, but what your friend may have neglected to tell you is to what wind direction the water is best suited. For example, nearly all locations on the south coast of England are hopeless in a northerly wind.

It can be very frustrating to leave home in perfect conditions only to arrive at the chosen beach with rain and an unfavourable wind. The weathermen are your best ally in making a good decision

and probably the best coastal forecasts are those provided by 'Marineline'. These forecasts are designed specifically for water users and provide a regional service throughout the UK. After a while you begin to be able to interpret the forecast for the sailing conditions in a particular region. Normally they forecast for open water so when they say its going to blow Force 3–4, the wind on the beach tends to be nearer Force 2–3. Excluding the sudden arrival of a frontal system, the wind direction is predictable and you can plan with a map the place most likely to have the ideal cross-shore winds which enable easy launching and recovery.

The greatest danger to a windsurfer is a wind that blows you away from a beach. You should never sail in an offshore wind, particularly not alone. An *offshore* wind will become progressively stronger the further you are blown out, and as you find you can't cope, you'll spend more and more time in the water, being pushed in a direction you don't want to go, at an ever increasing speed. If you have got yourself in this situation and cannot get back to the beach, drop your sail and try and attract attention, by waving the fluorescent flag you should be carrying. On no account should you leave your board.

An onshore wind will also be difficult as it builds up dumping waves with mast-breaking force. This makes launching hazardous for both equipment and sailor.

Arriving

When you arrive at the area you've chosen a useful first stop is the local windsurfing shop, the address of which should be advertised in the windsurfing press. Most shops have at least one windsurfing enthusiast, who should be happy to advise you further since you could become a future customer. Some shops will even be able to tell you over the phone exactly what the wind and waves are doing.

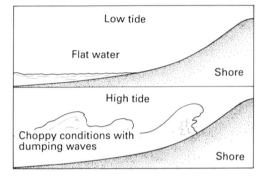

Fig 37 Low tide is always better for learning as the water is much flatter and any waves have little power. High tide is often positively dangerous, with vicious dumping waves breaking on the steep slope of the upper beach. Launching is very difficult. (*See also* fig 78, page 87.)

TIDES
(Fig 37)
If the windsurfing shop doesn't have a tide table, the local newsagent should. The time of high and low water is one of the most important things you should know, since not only does it affect the direction of any dangerous currents but also how flat the water will be.

Windsurfing during the two hours either side of high water is ill-advised on most beaches in all but the lightest winds. With the water high up on the beach the sea is very choppy and launching is very difficult because the waves break viciously on the steep upper slopes of the beach (which is frequently a shingle

ridge). On many beaches high tide brings the added danger of groynes. Even the best sailors can be swept into them, apart from which they can cause all sorts of damage to your equipment. I know someone who earns his living by repairing boards and he always does most business on the days after a strong onshore wind has combined with a high tide.

Some of Britain's most popular wind-surfing beaches are adjacent to the mouths of estuaries and rivers. The reason for this is that the outflowing rivers provide the sand that makes them good beaches. However, although rivers and estuaries helped to form these beaches, they also provide a major threat to those who windsurf from them. In the mouths of such harbours and rivers there are some very strong tidal currents that can catch out even the most skilful of sailors. When the tide flows out, the current often flows straight out to sea washing any distressed windsurfer with it. You should avoid any harbour entrances for this reason, as well as the probable use of the channel by other far larger craft, i.e. boats and ships.

OTHER SAILORS
The local sailors are the people who probably know the conditions best, so it is worth while speaking to someone who can point out the idiosyncrasies of the location. If there is a school or rescue service on the beach, then their advice will also be useful.

Setting Sail

Having arrived, there is every reason to be dubious if no one else is on the water: perhaps it is dangerous, or there is a better place close by. Whatever the

Setting off in More Wind

1. Use a fairly low body position immediately after you raise the rig; this will make it harder for you to be pulled over and with slightly bent legs you will be able to react to board wobble caused by waves.
2. Always exaggerate the pulling of the rig across you into the wind before applying the power with the back hand. This is also important at the end of tacking and gybing. (*See* fig 33.)

reason, you would be ill-advised to go out on your own.

Hopefully, however, there will be plenty of others sailing, and you can learn a lot by watching them for a while. By watching, waiting and chatting you should be able to evaluate the following points, which should be considered before you take to the water.

1. Sail selection. What size of sail will be comfortable? See what sailors of a similar weight and standard to yourself are using. If in doubt, it is always better to go out slightly underpowered and be able to get back, rather than struggle from the outset.
2. Tide and wind. Is your own information on the tide and wind predictions the same as the local sailors' interpretation?
3. What local tips are there? How can you avoid any rips or currents there might be? Are there any hidden obstructions such as sandbanks, rocks or wrecks that might claim your skeg or body if you run into them?
4. Restrictions. On some beaches there are bathing zones, shipping channels and waterski areas, which are often protected by bylaws to keep other water users out. Park and sail in the designated areas and respect other beach users, otherwise you could cause terrible problems for the local windsurfing community.
5. Recovery. If you broke something, how would you get back in and where would you drift to?
6. Can you handle the conditions? Although you might have driven a long way to get there, don't put yourself into a situation you can't handle. There will normally be another venue nearby where you can sail far more safely.

If the beach is crowded with swimmers, sail well clear of them since a board travelling even at low speed could do severe damage to someone's head. Also, although others may be wearing very little, you should always ensure that you are dressed sensibly for the occasion. It is far better to be too warm than too cold.

If you are considering doing any long-distance sailing, remember that distances over water are very deceptive. A number of boards have been rescued after trying to make the long sail from the English coast to the Isle of Wight, which on a clear day appears far closer than it actually is. For any long-distance sailing you should inform someone where you are going and when you expect to return. Sail with someone else and carry some means of attracting attention in the event of an accident, such as flares or a daglo flag.

As you can see, it is all a matter of common sense yet hundreds of windsurfers are rescued off the British coastline each year. Perhaps if you see anyone not using their sense you could do them and all other windsurfers a favour by telling them.

47

Collisions – Two Simple Rules

These days some sailing spots can become fairly busy at peak times. If it is windy boards can be travelling at high speeds and some nasty collisions have been known to occur. The two simple rules explained below will help you understand who should take avoiding action – they are common to boards and boats – but don't expect a big yacht to get out of your way if you're blasting flat out!

• A board on port tack keeps clear

When two boards are heading straight for one another they will often be on opposite tacks. The board on starboard tack, that is, the person whose right hand is next to the mast (board S in the diagram), will theoretically be in the 'right': port tack has to keep clear.

For those from a landlubber's background starboard is the right-hand side on the water (port = left) and a board which is sailing with the wind passing over its right-hand edge before hitting the sail is said to be sailing on a starboard tack (*see* diagram).

• A windward board should keep clear.

Now what if both boards are on the same tack? Expressed simply, the one that is closest to where the wind is coming from has to keep clear. In the diagram below this is board W.

There is another common sense rule attached to this which we all use when driving a car. If board W, 10 seconds before the situation shown in the diagram, was whizzing up to overtake board L, it would be common sense to expect W to keep clear. This indeed applies and 'an overtaking board should keep clear'.

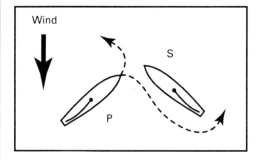

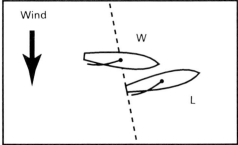

3
Introducing Planing Techniques

Windsurfing in stronger winds produces an exhilaration and satisfaction that is difficult to equal. For a while though, I had a psychological block to sailing in fresher winds because I thought my weight and strength was not up to it. I also hated being beaten by the wind and was frustrated by my lack of progress. It was not until I saw a sailor much smaller than myself performing in a Force 6 that it dawned on me that the answer must lie in a good technique.

STANCE
(Figs 38 to 40)

The beginner's stance needs to be altered to handle higher winds otherwise you will

Key Points
As the wind increases, hand and feet positions should move further back; your arms should be extended, with shoulders and hips parallel to the sail. Lean with your weight rather than pulling with your arms.

Working down the body we can pin-point the individual aspects of an efficient stance.

Fig 38 Here the CE is marked and the hands are spaced equally either side of it. The arms are straight, placing the strain on the larger groups of shoulder and back muscles. Notice how the shoulders are parallel to the boom whilst the hips, knees and feet are all facing the direction of 'pull', making for the most efficient sailing position.

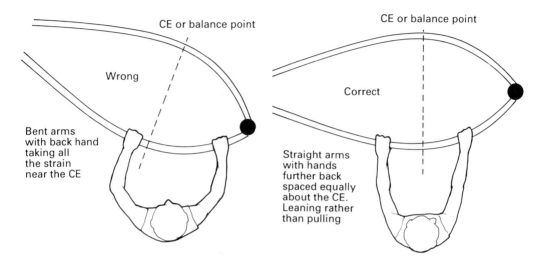

Fig 39   Strong wind stance – hand positions.

tire quickly and the boom will constantly be ripped from your grasp.

HEAD

This faces forwards in the direction of travel looking for gusts and lulls; it should look over the front shoulder and not under the armpit. By spotting any wind changes in advance, the body can anticipate their arrival and compensate.

SHOULDERS

They should remain roughly parallel to the sail, hence their angle will depend on your course of sailing.

ARMS

These should be extended with the elbows facing down, and the front arm in particular should be straight. Bent arms become tired far quicker than straight arms.

HANDS
(Fig 39)

The correct hand position is vital. They should be about shoulder-width apart, placed equidistant from the CE so that there is an equal amount of strain on both arms. If the hands are too far forwards, as is often the case, the back arm being so close to the CE cannot take all the strain and tends to sheet out causing the board to turn into the wind.

LEGS

The legs should be slightly bent, with the knees supple and ready to straighten or bend to absorb rough water.

FEET

These must follow the example of the hands and move back down the board as the wind increases. Remember that the front foot faces forwards. Feet placed

OTHER CONSIDERATIONS

Starting

A common problem when starting in stronger winds is that the board seems constantly to turn into the wind. This is caused by the steering properties of a sail only partly sheeted in. The sail should be pulled well across the body and then swiftly sheeted in. The secret is to lean back hard as you apply the power. You can't hold back here – you have to trust that the power from the sail will pull you back up again should you lean too far. A low body position will also help.

Apparent Wind
(Fig 41)

If you run in still air the *apparent wind* you feel blows in your face. In stronger winds, by moving through the water quickly we create more wind. So, on a board the apparent wind we experience when we travel at 10 knots in a 10 knot cross-wind will be a 14 knot wind hitting us at 45 degrees.

What this means is that the faster we go, the more the apparent wind direction swings forwards. So, in strong winds the sail has to be sheeted in far tighter than in light winds. When speed sailors sail at high speeds (45+ knots is the current record) they have their sails in a close hauled position although they are sailing on a broad reach.

The Catapult Fall
(Fig 42)

This spectacular fall happens when a gust of wind hits the sail and you are thrown off your feet over the boom. It is an

direction of 'pull'

shoulders, hips and feet all uniform

Fig 40   Former European Champion Jane Clague makes it look so easy in a Force 4; and she's smiling! As opposed to the beginner's posture, her weight is doing all the work. This is possible since hands and feet are considerably further back with shoulders, hips and feet all pointing in the direction that the sail is pulling in. There is no twisting or unevenness in her gait. Notice how the backside is slightly dropped into a sitting position – 80 per cent of the pull is taken through the harness. If the board were not as level as it is, it would start turning.

wide apart may feel more stable, but only encourage a pulling action rather than leaning.

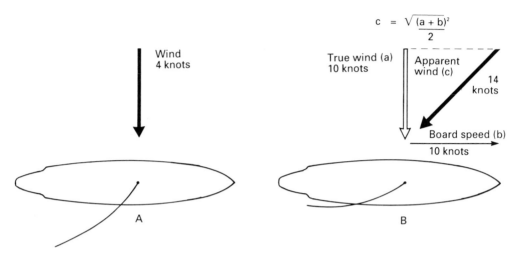

$$c = \sqrt{\frac{(a + b)^2}{2}}$$

Wind
4 knots

True wind (a)
10 knots

Apparent
wind (c)
14 knots

Board speed (b)
10 knots

A

B

Fig 41 Apparent wind. Board A is tethered and the true and apparent winds are the same. Board B is moving at 10 knots in a 10 knot cross-wind. The resulting apparent wind blows at 45 degrees and the sail has to be sheeted in tightly.

Fig 42 Even the best sailors sometimes take catapult falls. Here it probably happened by sailing into the steep wave resulting in a sudden loss of speed. To avoid being thrown when sailing in waves, look ahead to choose the best course and allow the knees to flex over the waves.

indication that your weight is too far forward and to avoid it the feet should be positioned further back and more weight should be placed on the back foot.

Land Practice

A great deal can be practised on land by removing the skeg and placing the board in a suitable position with clear wind. Experiment with different hand and feet positions and try and get used to the idea of leaning back on a straight front arm. This is also a good place to practise strong wind starting, but you should have a colleague to support the sail if it falls.

USING THE FOOTSTRAPS

Footstraps are on the board to stop your feet bouncing or being washed off in stronger winds. They have no use until the board reaches planing speed, and for

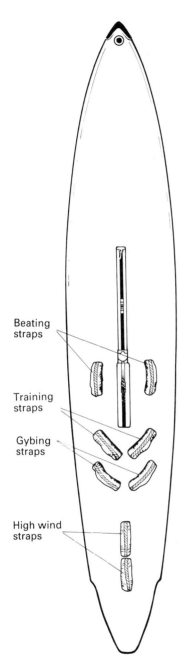

Beating straps

Training straps

Gybing straps

High wind straps

Fig 43   A typical footstrap arrangement on an all-round funboard of more than 3.50m.

novices and light wind sailing they are best removed.

Adjustment

It is important that you set the straps for your own foot size. They must fit tightly across the top of the foot. *Too loose* and your foot and ankle could slide all the way through after a fall, possibly resulting in a broken leg. *Too tight* and your toes will be cramped. This will cause both feet to rest on the windward rail, making it difficult to keep the board level. Your back foot should be far enough in the back strap to straddle the centreline of the board.

Remember to adjust the straps at the beginning and end of the season to accommodate either bare feet or boots.

Strap Positions
(Fig 43)

Beating straps are only occasionally fitted to race boards and, as the name suggests, their sole use is for sailing into wind. With the track forwards, the front or back foot can be placed in the strap. Some people prefer not to use them at all and remove them.

The next pair are the training straps, which are used in the early stages to accustom sailors to footstrap use. For very heavy sailors, however, these might prove to be the most suitable straps as putting the weight further back might sink the tail of the board.

Behind these come what I call the gybing straps, since these are used during the carve gybe, and at the back of the board are the two high wind straps, which can only be used in Force 4 or above.

Boards under 3.00m in length normally use only the gybing and high wind straps.

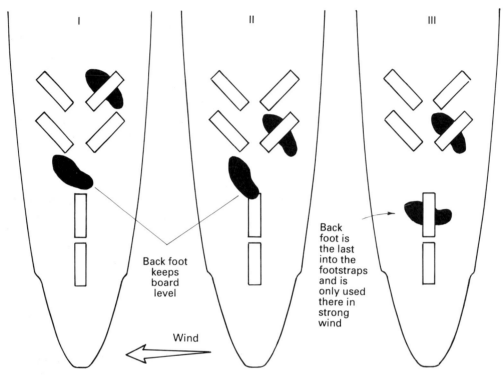

I   II   III

Back foot
keeps
board
level

Back
foot is
the last
into the
footstraps
and is
only used
there in
strong
wind

Wind

Fig 44 Getting into the footstraps. Transfer your weight through the boom on to the mastfoot.

Key Points
Ensure that the board is planing; front foot is first into the training strap; transfer your body weight through the mastfoot as you move back; move further back as the wind increases.
Wind Force 3 +
Mast Track Middle to back
Daggerboard Retracted

Getting into the Straps

Many people, in order to feel more secure, make the mistake of diving into the straps at the first possible opportunity. Think of your board as a speedboat. As you open up the throttle, you need to move to the front of the boat to help it to rise on to the plane. Once it is planing, you can move back again. As you start, therefore, concentrate on keeping the board level and getting it to move as quickly as possible.

SEQUENCE
1. Get the board moving as fast as possible with the centreboard retracted.
2. Place your front foot in the training strap, using the back foot to keep the board level.
3. When wind or board speed increases sufficiently, place the front foot in the

gybing strap, again using the back foot for stability.

4. Place your back foot in the front high wind strap.

5. If speed is lost, quickly move forwards on the board.

It is important to think of the high wind straps as being completely independent of the straps further forward. Thus, it does *not* follow that if one foot is in the training strap, the other must use the front high wind strap.

Faults

A common complaint is that the straps are too far back and that the board keeps turning into the wind. The reasons for this are:

1. Not having an efficient strong wind stance. (This is the most common fault.)
2. Attempting to use the straps when the wind is not strong enough.
3. The centreboard being down.
4. Not using the above sequence.
5. Not keeping the board level with the back foot.
6. The footstraps being too tight, causing all the weight to fall on the windward side.
7. Not transferring your weight on to the mastfoot.

Footsteering

Footsteering is best practised in position C of the sequence and only when the board is planing fast. With the daggerboard retracted, the board can be steered solely by weight movements and behaves like a surfboard, water-ski or skateboard, in that if you weight one side of the board it will turn in that direction.

By rocking back on your heels, the weight will be transferred to the windward side and the board will turn into the wind. To bear away from the wind, you must move your body weight to the other side by bending the knees and bringing the hips over the board. The best practice is to try steering a controlled wiggly course using your weight. To do this you will need to move your back foot.

Remember as you head up and bear away that the sail will need to be sheeted in and out accordingly, otherwise the board will stop. If the board fails to respond to your weight, this is an indication that either you are not travelling fast enough or your weight is not far enough back on the board.

THE HARNESS

The harness takes the strain off your arms and allows you to stay out on the water far longer. Rather than weary arms taking the strain, the harness lines do, allowing maximum use of body weight whilst letting the arms make fine adjustments to the sail. More and more people are learning the basics of harness use in as little as 8 knots.

Harnesses have progressed a lot from the early designs of the 1970s, and there are now three different types in use.

1. The *waistcoat harness*. This conventional harness has a fairly high hook position, which is still used by some wave sailors. It is becoming less popular now because of the lack of support it gives to the lower back, although it does give more buoyancy than other types.
2. The *waist harness*. This is widely used because of the comfort and lack of restriction of the upper body.

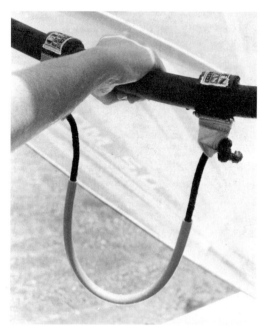 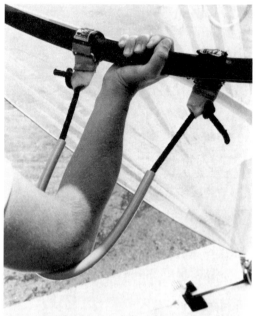

Fig 45   As a guide to where to fix the harness lines adopt a sailing position with the rig on the beach and try to find the balance point on the boom by moving your hands closer together or by using only one hand. Once you have a feel for where this balance point is, set up the harness attachments equidistantly either side of this point. A shoulder width apart is a good width.

Fig 46   As a very rough guide to harness depth or line length use your forearm in this way. You may notice that racers often have shorter lines than this.

Setting up the Lines
(Figs 45 to 48)

3. The *seat harness*. This can take many forms, but the idea is that part of it is strapped around your backside; this prevents the hook from riding up and allows you to take all the weight of the rig by sitting. It is commonly used in racing and flat water sailing.

The ideal learning conditions for getting acquainted with the harness are flat water with a Force 2 to 3 onshore wind. Gusty winds are to be avoided at all costs.

This is very important since lines that are either the wrong length or not balanced can provoke a string of problems including tired arms, aching backs, bad posture and catapult falls.

The lines are positioned by referring to the CE or balance point of the rig. On most sails this imaginary point lies about 18 to 22 inches (46 to 56cm) from the front of the boom and can be found by standing the rig on the beach in a steady wind.

A good way to check the lines are in the correct position ĭs to temporarily release one or both hands from the boom whilst hooked in. If the lines are balanced you

Fig 47   Harness designs vary in their detail but this seat harness is a common and effective design. You should select a harness that feels comfortable to wear in the shop. If there is any control strap that lowers the hook position have this fairly slack when learning to use it; you don't want the hook to be so low that hooking in is difficult, so a higher position is preferable to start with.

should be able to hold this position for a few seconds without the sail changing its position.

The 'depth' of the lines is equally as important as the positioning and it should be such that the arms can be almost extended when hooked in.

Hooking In and Out

When on a close reach, hook in by pulling the rig sharply towards you and letting the line swing up to meet your hook. A hip movement towards the swinging line will also help, but beware of moving the *whole* body towards the sail as this will encourage a catapult fall.

You can unhook simply by taking the weight of the rig back on to your arms,

thereby allowing the rope to fall out of the hook.

Faults

Difficulty in hooking in can sometimes be attributed to harness lines that are too short. The commonest problem, though, is the balance of the lines. If you feel excess pressure on your front arm, move the line towards the mast, and vice versa if the back arm seems overworked.

Do not attempt to use the harness on a run as it is difficult to control the gusts.

THE MAST TRACK

The mast track is now a common feature

Fig 48   Look, no hands! Peter Hart showing how perfectly balanced lines take all the strain out of sailing. You can clearly see how far back the lines are positioned on this 6.5 sq m. sail in a Force 5.

on most boards and with proper use it can increase the board's speed and man-oeuvrability, particularly in stronger winds. Only competent windsurfers can take advantage of the mast track, so if you are still mastering other techniques it is best to leave it in the middle and forget about it.

Moving the Track

Most tracks are operated by a pedal which, when depressed, enables adjust-ment. With the front foot on the pedal, the track is moved forwards by pushing downwards on the boom and backwards

by pulling up on the boom. This will only work with the rig inclined back in the sailing position, otherwise it may be necessary to use one hand on the mast.

Positioning

A lot of confusion surrounds the 'where and when' of mast track positioning. The simplest approach is to look at it as a device that moves your weight up and down the board. So, with it at the front the board lies on the water flat, and with it back the tail digs in.

For a board over 3.20m there are three positions in which you can use the mast track: towards the front, towards the back or in the middle. For shorter boards the same principles apply, but the back position does not make the board faster as the board planes on too small a surface and becomes difficult to control.

FRONT

The track is used in the front position for sailing into wind, as nearly all the length of the board is in the water and this provides the greatest sideways resistance.

BACK

The back position can only be properly used in strong winds on a reach; in lighter winds the board will just sit on its tail causing lots of drag. Once there is enough wind to plane, though, the back position comes into its own, since with the weight back only a small amount of the board is in contact with the water thus enabling high speeds. Also, with less length of board in the water, the board becomes more manoeuvrable (just as a short car has a tighter lock than a long estate model).

MIDDLE

The middle position is used for reaching in medium winds as it prevents the tail from digging in too much and encourages the board to plane. This is the best all-round position.

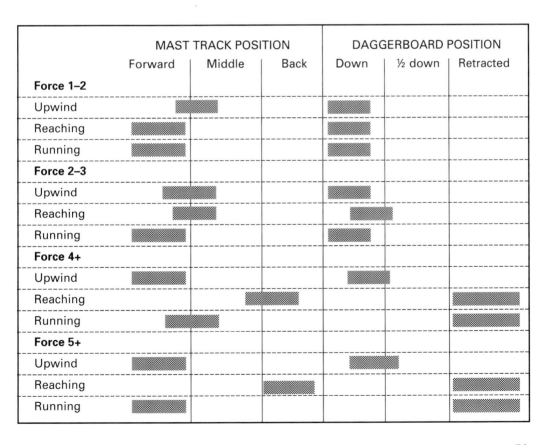

	MAST TRACK POSITION			DAGGERBOARD POSITION		
	Forward	Middle	Back	Down	½ down	Retracted
Force 1–2						
Upwind	▨			▨		
Reaching	▨			▨		
Running	▨			▨		
Force 2–3						
Upwind	▨			▨		
Reaching		▨			▨	
Running	▨			▨		
Force 4+						
Upwind	▨				▨	
Reaching		▨				▨
Running	▨					▨
Force 5+						
Upwind	▨				▨	
Reaching			▨			▨
Running	▨					▨

4
Funboard Technique

The funboard skills in this chapter draw heavily on good strong wind technique, and you should be able to sail comfortably in moderate to strong winds and use the harness and footstraps without mishap before attempting what follows. It does not follow that in owning a funboard you should only learn funboard techniques.

Funboard Requirements

The following six points form the essentials of funboard sailing and set a good funboard sailor apart from a bad one.

COMMITMENT
Commitment, or a 'go for it' attitude as windsurfers have termed it, is perhaps the most essential ingredient of all. When you have a high level of commitment your attention is focused specifically on what you've chosen to do and the way you've chosen to do it. You cannot be tentative or apprehensive in your movements; you have to throw caution to the wind and 'attack' a manoeuvre with the objective clearly fixed in your mind.

MOBILITY
Funboard sailing by its very nature requires more agility and suppleness than is needed in light winds. Warming up is a good idea, especially in colder conditions.

TIMING
Everything happens so much quicker in stronger winds, so a good sense of timing is needed. This is gradually learned so that, for instance, you know exactly when to gybe in choppy water to take advantage of the waves.

EFFICIENT STANCE
This is not so much an attribute but a requirement since, as we shall see later, it is essential for any of the more complicated techniques, as it provides the necessary speed.

UPRIGHT RIG
Keeping an upright rig also distinguishes a good funboard sailor since it gives more forward drive whilst sailing and more lift in beach and water starts.

BODY WEIGHT
By using body weight through the mastfoot a good sailor will water start and sail his board more efficiently than a bad one.

STANCE

The posture for funboard sailing is no different from that required for any other board, apart from the fact that the feet are commonly in the footstraps. However, nearly all funboard technique problems can be traced back to deficiencies in the strong wind stance. The most common cause is that of the front hand being too far forward on the boom, which causes luffing problems in the water start and the beach start and gives insufficient speed in the carve gybe. The strong wind stance described earlier is the basis of the funboard stance, but to it we can add a further ingredient – the hips and bottom.

Try this: with a partner of equal weight try pulling each other over with hands clasped and toes touching. Stop! The first thing you do is drop your bottom and push with your legs to make use of your weight. Some people use this instinctively in their windsurfing in stronger winds and especially now that seat and waist harnesses are widely used. It is a particularly useful method of sailing in gusty conditions where the hips can move in and out to compensate for the fluctuations in the wind without moving the sail. So, although you are discouraged from dropping your bottom as a beginner, it is very useful when the wind increases in handling the extra pull (as Fig 40 demonstrated).

The important points to re-emphasise from stronger wind stance are that the hands and feet should move back as the wind increases to centre around the balance point. Also the arms, and in particular the front one, should be straight since not only is this less tiring but it keeps the rig upright and provides more power. Finally, the head should point forwards while the other parts of the body remain square to the sail.

THE BEACH START
(Figs 49 to 52)

The beach start enables you to step on to

> **Key Points**
> Mastfoot pressure; back foot on centreline; upright rig; straight front arm.
> *Wind* Force 1 to 6
> *Mast track* Middle
> *Daggerboard* Retracted

your board without having to haul the sail out of the water. It becomes compulsory when sailing off exposed beaches in rough conditions, since it means you can escape the hazardous shorebreak quickly.

Strictly speaking, this is not solely a funboard technique but I include it here as it has such close links with the water start.

Tips

MANOEUVRING INTO POSITION
This is done by applying pressure to the mastfoot by pulling or pushing with one hand on the mast. The board will pivot around the skeg. The sail should not be powered until you are ready to go.

THE BACK FOOT
It is imperative that this is placed on the centreline otherwise the board will swiftly turn into the wind once any weight is put on it. If you have difficulty keeping the board on a broad reach, you can use the back foot to draw the board towards you.

GETTING GOING
Let the wind do the work and pull you up on to the board. You will only get enough power to do this by extending the arms as high as possible, thereby getting the rig upright. If when you get on all your weight is left on the back foot, the back of the board will inevitably sink and you will go

THE BEACH START

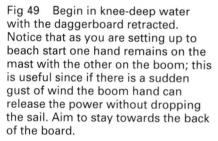

Fig 49   Begin in knee-deep water with the daggerboard retracted. Notice that as you are setting up to beach start one hand remains on the mast with the other on the boom; this is useful since if there is a sudden gust of wind the boom hand can release the power without dropping the sail. Aim to stay towards the back of the board.

Fig 50   By applying pressure through the mastfoot you can manoeuvre the board into position. Pulling up on the rig will turn the board into the wind whilst pushing it away from you will turn the front away from the board. The board is pivoting around the skeg when you do this. The ideal starting position is a broad reach (*see* fig 22).

Fig 51 *(opposite, top)*   When you're ready to go, transfer both hands on to the boom and place your back foot on to the board. If footstraps are fitted, place the foot in front of the rear set of straps; the heavier you are the further forward you will need to place this foot to prevent the tail sinking too much. It is important to place the foot on the centreline and draw the back of the board towards you by using the heel.

Fig 52 *(opposite, bottom)*   By pulling the board ever closer to you and extending your arms and shoulders forwards you should be able to step up on to the board using mostly strong leg power, the right leg in this instance. It is only in stronger winds that the power from the sail does the work of getting you on to the board. Light-wind beach starts such as the one shown here are the easiest way of setting off. As you step forward on to the board release the power in the sail slightly; this stops you from being pulled forwards. In stronger winds far more power control is needed with the sail throughout this whole sequence.

for a swim – so as you step on to the board move your weight forwards quickly.

Fault Finding

'The board keeps on turning into wind as I get going.' There are a number of possible causes of this:

1. Board is not in correct starting position.
2. Not having your weight on the centre-line.
3. Sheeting out as you step up.
4. Not moving your weight forwards quickly enough.

'I can't seem to get close enough to the board to get my foot on.' Possible reasons for this include:

1. Approaching the board from side-on rather than from the rear quarter.
2. Not lifting the boom high enough above you; control the extra power by spilling wind.

THE WATER START

Of all the skills in windsurfing water starting is the most highly prized as it opens the door to a whole range of smaller high performance boards. Uphauling in stronger winds, as well as being extremely difficult, is very tiring and often frustrating. The water start uses the force of the wind to pull you out of the water and, when performed properly, is a faster and more efficient means of starting on all types of board. Even on a raceboard with a 7.5 sq m. sail, the water start is used in strong winds after a fall since it is so much quicker.

There are many similarities with beach starting, indeed many people have taught themselves by performing increasingly deeper versions of the beach start. The water start is divided into two parts: the rig recovery and the start itself.

All lengths of board can be used provided they can support your weight, but when learning the sail should not be larger than 6.0 sq m and should have a boom length shorter than 2.00m.

Try to use a sail with a narrow luff tube and definitely *not* a camber-induced sail. To help you float higher in the water and save energy it can be worth using a buoyancy aid.

Rig Recovery
(Figs 53 to 57)

Key Points
Position mast at 90 degrees to the wind; swim vigorously into the wind; pull rig diagonally upwards and into the wind.
Wind Force 3 minimum
Mast Track Middle to back
Daggerboard Retracted

This is undoubtedly the most tiring skill to learn since it involves so much swimming. The aim is to arrange the rig at right angles to the wind so the wind can blow under it, allowing the sail to fly.

TIPS
1. Aligning the mast to 90 degrees (Fig 53) Obviously the rig does not always conveniently lie in this position for you, so you must swim the rig into position with a strong leg action.

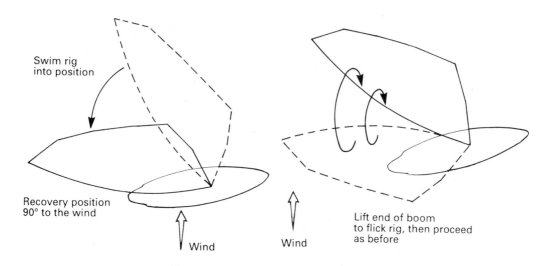

Swim rig
into position

Recovery position
90° to the wind

Wind

Wind

Lift end of boom
to flick rig, then proceed
as before

Fig 53   Aligning the rig.

Let the rig 'flip'

WIND

Fig 54   Flipping the rig into a better position. By lifting the end of the boom
the wind will catch under the sail and flip it over. Kick hard with legs and spare
hand.

65

Fig 55   Raising the rig.

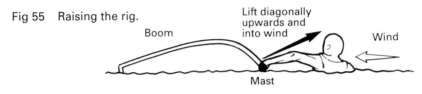

(Viewed from mast tip)

Sometimes, though, the rig falls in an awkward position, in which case the rig has to be flipped by lifting the end of the boom. For first attempts the board is best positioned as above, but with practice the board can be manoeuvred once the rig is out of the water.

2. *Raising the rig* (Figs 55 and 56)   The main points here are to swim vigorously into wind, which will help release the water off the back of the sail, and lift the sail upwards and diagonally into wind. When raising the rig one hand is on the mast, whilst the other treads water helping the feet.

3. *Controlling the rig*   Once the rig is free the hands move on to the boom in the normal sailing position and the power is controlled by sheeting in and out.

FAULT FINDING

'The back of the sail seems to dig into the water as I raise the rig.' Possible causes of this are:

1. Not swimming hard into the wind.
2. Lifting vertically up, rather than into the wind.

If this happens, pull down on the mast hard and swim into the wind.

Fig 56   Rig recovery. Once the rig is at 90 degrees to the wind, swim hard upwind and lift the rig diagonally which will let the wind under the sail.

Fig 57 Here the clew of the sails has caught in the water because the mast has been raised too high. When this happens, swim vigorously into wind and pull down hard on the mast.

The Start
(Figs 58 to 61)

> **Key Points**
> Pull the board close to you by using the back foot; maintain an upright rig; kick hard with the front foot; lean forwards applying weight to mastfoot.
>
> It is a common fallacy that the wind does all the work in a water start by pulling you on to the board. In fact, in winds of Force 3 to 5 it only does about half the work in getting your weight over the back foot, the rest is up to you. Only in very strong winds does it pull you completely out of the water.

TIPS
1. Get close to the board (Fig 58) By using the back heel placed on the centre-line, pull the back of the board towards you thereby making it infinitely easier for the rig to pull you over the board.

2. Extend your arms Keep them well down the boom to get the rig as upright as possible.

3. Kick hard with your front leg Unless you have very large feet you won't get much extra lift, but it will help your stability and balance.

4. Lean forwards as you rise As in the beach start, by leaning down on a straight front arm you are taking the weight off the back of the board and putting it on the mastfoot.

FAULT FINDING
'I keep heading into wind when I try starting.' Possible causes of this are:

1. Not starting on a reach; remember – use the back foot to bring the back of the board towards you.

67

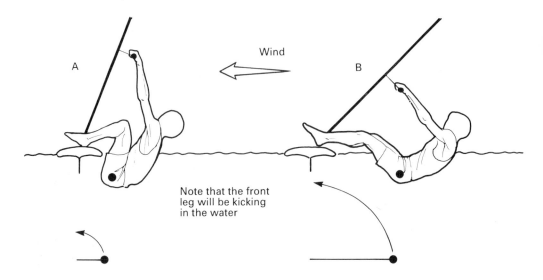

Fig 58   This illustrates the importance of getting close to the board. A has used his back foot to pull the board closer to him, thereby making it far easier to pull himself up. Note how much more upright his rig is compared to B's, and also that by being further underneath the boom, it is easier to apply pressure to the mastfoot. Note that it is the heel which rests on the board, not the whole foot.

Fig 59   The water start. Once the rig is free, transfer the hands to a position well back on the boom. Kick hard with your feet and position yourself by the rear quarter of the board.

Fig 60   Extend the rig well above you with straight arms as in the beach start. This not only supplies more power, but also enables you to get close enough to the board to put your foot on it. Notice the back heel is placed on the centreline and, again like the beach start, can be used to bring the board closer. Keep the spare leg kicking hard; this supplies a little lift and also stops the board's rapid progress sideways.

As you rise, lean forwards transferring your weight on to the mast foot

Fig 61   As you rise up lean well forwards; this will transfer much of your weight through the front arm on to the mast foot. Kick the front leg vigorously as if you were trying to attract a shark! Notice how the compact legs are enabling the body to keep close to the board.

2. Not having the weight on the centre-line.

3. Not leaning forwards as you rise.

4. Not having a good enough strong wind stance.

'In very strong winds I can't prevent the sail from lifting me out of the water.'

1. To control the power keep the sail low and close to the water to decrease its effective area and slide one or both feet into the straps whilst lying in the water.

EXERCISE

As mentioned earlier, making deeper and deeper beach starts is often a successful way of tackling the water start, provided you have a gently shelving beach.

Another good way of practising the start without having to go through the exhausting rig recovery is to sail along and lower yourself into the water. In light winds this can still be done by lowering yourself to sit on the board and then pulling on a straight front arm to pull yourself up. It develops the idea of using weight through the mastfoot.

THE CARVE GYBE
(Figs 62 to 66)

> **Key Points**
> Approach with speed; weight the inside rail; sheet in with the back hand; drive with the knees; keep the rig forward and in front of you; timing of feet and rig change.
> *Wind* Force 4+, flat water
> *Mast Track* Towards the back
> *Daggerboard* Retracted

This is the most satisfying of all manoeuvres since with enough speed and with the daggerboard retracted the board is turned like a surfboard or ski by weighting the inside edge. A good stance and plenty of wind is needed to get sufficient speed and then the footsteering principle is used throughout the turn with little help from the sail.

Equipment and Location

Although all lengths of board will carve gybe, the longer all-round funboards need a higher level of skill than the more responsive 3.30m size of board which is ideally suited to first attempts. The sail size needs to be large enough to get you planing at speed. Here we shall deal with the basic carve gybe on a board over 3.00m. Shorter boards have slightly different techniques.

A flat water venue is vital since choppy coastal conditions make smooth turns very difficult, even for the experts. Imagine learning to water-ski on the sea with waves – you wouldn't be making life easy for yourself.

Tips

FOOT PLACEMENT
(Fig 62)

You can only turn properly if you are using the gybing straps. The back foot is placed on the leeward side of the board with a number of factors (such as the weight of the sailor and the length of the board) determining where you place it. At first, place your foot in position with very little weight on it; then, when you decide to begin the turn, swing your body weight across the board by bending the knees so that more and more weight is borne on

70

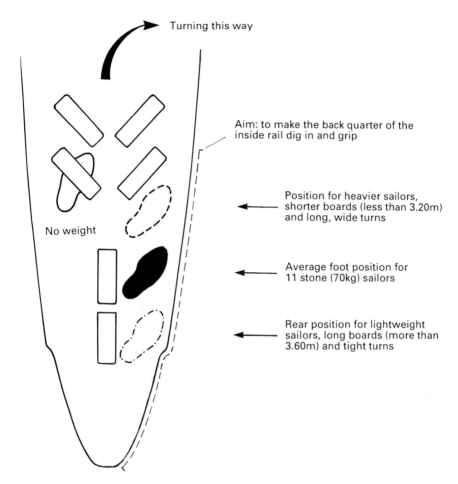

Turning this way

Aim: to make the back quarter of the inside rail dig in and grip

Position for heavier sailors, shorter boards (less than 3.20m) and long, wide turns

Average foot position for 11 stone (70kg) sailors

Rear position for lightweight sailors, long boards (more than 3.60m) and tight turns

No weight

Fig 62   Foot placement variables in the carve gybe.

the back foot. In mid-turn *all* the weight will be on the inside foot whilst the other remains in the strap. When placing weight on the feet, use the front of the feet and toes rather than the heels. The main thing is to concentrate on a smooth rig change since as soon as novices start stomping their feet around the board the banking angle is lost and the turn fails. Normally then, rig first feet later.

BODY POSITION

The key to a good carve gybe is committing your body weight to the inside of the turn. Your ankles need to be flexible to enable the knees to bend and drive towards the inside of the turn; try to bend your knees so they touch the foot of the sail. It is this weight alteration, or rocking action, which initiates the carving position.

Hips and shoulders should be over the centreline of the board with a straight

71

THE CARVE GYBE

Fig 63   Fig 64

Fig 63   Whilst approaching on a reach look for the flattest piece of water and start bearing away to gain speed. Slide the back hand down the boom then unhook and check downwind for any other boards. Keep bearing away, once you have gained full speed remove the back foot from the strap and place it across the centreline. Do not sheet out, if anything you need to sheet in as the apparent wind comes forward (*see* fig 66c).

Fig 64   As you reach terminal velocity sway your hips and hence your weight on to the inside leg (in this case the left leg). Notice how bent both knees are and how the body is facing the sail. With the sail sheeted in, the rig can be leant into the turn, giving the impression that it is fixed to the board. With board and rig banked into the turn the front arm is extended to keep the rig away from you. You should be able to see the front of the board.

Fig 65   As the downwind position is approached there is very little wind in the sail. Note how the end of the boom would catch if it were not sheeted in. You can also see how the shoulders are rolled forwards. Looking at the feet we can see the heel is lifted off the board as all the weight is placed on the front of each foot.

Fig 66a   Now with the rig still relatively light (low apparent wind) the rig change is started. In this example we are about two-thirds of the way through the turn; in stronger winds it would be done far earlier. Whilst learning it is best to concentrate on experimenting with the timing of this rig change and not to worry too much about your feet.

Fig 65

Fig 66a

Fig 66b *(Right)* The sail has now been released with the back hand and this will be placed on the mast. (Figs 32 and 33 show how the rig is pulled vigorously into wind before sheeting in.) Miraculously the feet seemed to have changed position without us seeing it! Since this is a relatively light wind turn it happened earlier to keep the board planing; look how far forward the sailor has moved them, at least six inches in front of the straps; this is sometimes called a step gybe since it involves a large step forwards. Normally with more wind you can change feet and rig simultaneously.

front arm. This leading arm keeps the rig forward and at arm's length in front of you, vital for a good rig flip. Avoid at all costs a straight front leg, which is a sure sign that you are performing the fatal mistake of leaning too far back.

THE RIG

Imagine the mast is glued to the board, so that as the board banks into the turn, the mast does too. Moving the back hand back to sheet in and pushing the front arm forwards helps keep your weight forwards with shoulders facing into the turn.

TIMING

Help yourself as much as you can by looking ahead and picking the flattest piece of water in which to turn. Gybing in gusts will give you more speed.

The feet and rig positions change as you approach the new broad reach; do it earlier in extreme conditions. The feet normally change first – this flattens the board and helps maintain speed. The best guideline for timing is to move when the rig feels at its lightest; of course the faster you are going the lighter it feels.

APPARENT WIND THROUGH A CARVE GYBE

(Fig 66c)

It is useful to look at what the apparent wind does through a carve gybe. (Look at fig 41 for an explanation of apparent wind.) The calculations in the diagram have been based on a good sailor doing a gybe in 20 knots of wind in flat water. He enters the turn doing 21 and exits at 16 knots. Each dot represents a 30 degree increment through the arc of the turn with the arrows representing the strength and direction of the resulting apparent wind.

At position A, in 20 knots a good sailor

should be able to go faster than the wind, say 21 knots, with a staggering 29 knots of apparent wind.

At B the board speed increases as you bear away, but notice how the apparent wind moves further forwards; this continues at C. No wonder then that those who do not sheet in through a high-speed turn lose speed dramatically.

At the downwind position D there is actually 2 knots of wind blowing into your face. This is why top racers sometimes use the lay down of the rig to tuck it out of the way so it does not slow them down; they sheet in hard and lay it into the turn partly behind them. This is when the rig is at its lightest and the rig change is best started between here and position E.

As you can see, by position F the apparent wind is back up to a healthy 19 knots from a rather inconvenient direction. Rig changes done too late often look and feel clumsy because of this. The overall message is: sheet in hard, allow the board to accelerate to top speed and do the rig change before you get too far through the turn.

FAULT FINDING

'The board turns well to start with but then I just head off downwind.'

1. Not enough speed.
2. This is an indication that the weight has moved off the back part of the board and allowed the rails to dig in further forwards. Keep the body weight applied to the back part of the inside rail throughout the turn.

'I keep falling in on the inside of the turn.'

1. Avoid applying the weight to the turn by leaning the whole body, rather let the

74

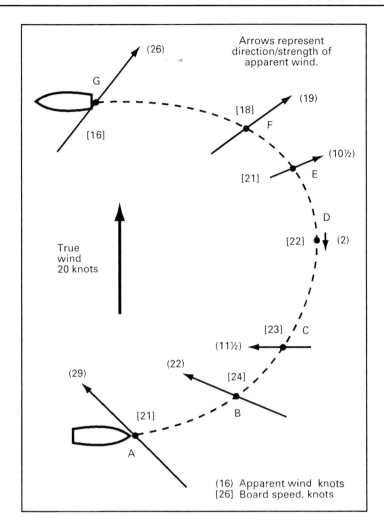

Fig 66c   Apparent wind through a carve gybe.

bent knees do the work whilst the upper body remains upright.

EXERCISES

Rather than trying to tackle the gybe as a whole, break it down into smaller component parts and try and make each part smooth. The rig change often deserves the greatest attention. The best way to perfect this is to do numerous light wind gybes since the technique is the same but everything happens much more slowly.

For all parts of the gybe proceed on a trial and error basis with different arcs of turn, different back foot placements and in particular changes in the timing.

A final word: do the carve gybe in flat water – it is so much easier, honestly!

75

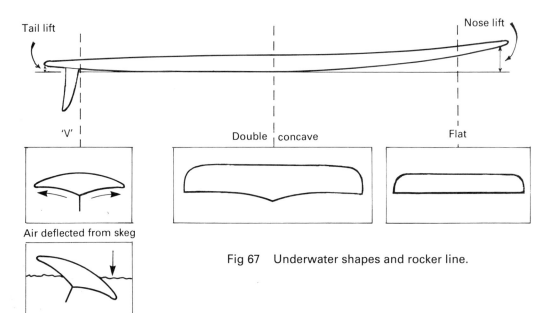

Air deflected from skeg

Only one edge can dig in

Fig 67 Underwater shapes and rocker line.

FUNBOARD DESIGN FEATURES

A lot of aggressive publicity and marketing surrounds funboard design, and for the uninitiated it is difficult to understand what is going on. Here then, cutting through all the waffle, is a concise run-down of what makes a board work.

Underwater Shapes
(Fig 67)

In an attempt to make the board plane in marginal winds (Force 3–4) some boards have single or double concaves. These subtle curves encourage air to flow under the board which gives extra lift and better acceleration. They were first developed on seaplanes to encourage them to take off at lower speeds and are now a common feature on speedboats. However, concaves are not used on speed- or race-orientated small boards where flat clean simple lines have been found to produce the best results.

Towards the back of the board is a characteristic known as 'V'. This encourages decisive footsteering since as one rail is depressed the other is raised. It also deflects unwanted air from passing the skeg which, as we shall see, is important at high speeds.

Skegs
(Fig 68)

There is an unbelievable variety of skeg shapes available which all aim to do the same job, namely keep the board sailing in a straight line. The huge variety of shapes is partly fashion and partly an attempt to avoid a phenomenon known as *spin out*. At very high speeds in Force 5+ a spin out occurs when the skeg suddenly stops working and the board loses control, slipping sideways. In fact, it feels

76

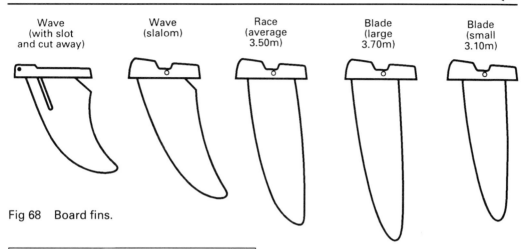

| Wave (with slot and cut away) | Wave (slalom) | Race (average 3.50m) | Blade (large 3.70m) | Blade (small 3.10m) |

Fig 68   Board fins.

Choosing a Fin

Whilst it is important to realise that fin choice can have a major influence on your effectiveness and fun, beware of the hype and bear the following points in mind:

1. A larger fin will promote earlier planing by providing something for the power of the sail to act against and will help get you upwind when you need to.

2. A fin that is too upright will hinder learning how to carve gybe. The more upright the leading edge, the flatter the board is meant to be sailed to optimise fin performance, consequently the more difficult it is to gybe. An upright fin tends to engage more of a board's rails.

3. A good fit in the fin box is absolutely vital. There are several items on the market that can enhance a good, tight fit.

4. Placing the fin further back in the box will give the board more directional stability whilst positioning it forwards will make the board easier to turn; however, there is a risk that by placing it forwards spin out may occur more readily.

as if the skeg has dropped off. What happens is that on a high speed reach there is so much sideways pressure on the skeg that an area of low pressure around the skeg sucks air down and creates an air pocket around the fin, therefore making it useless. Spin out also occurs after landing badly from a jump.

In an attempt to cure spin out (and sell more skegs) the manufacturers have come out with a number of ingenious shapes over the years. The *fenced* fin was first, followed by the strangely shaped *football* fin. These designs are now dated largely because they didn't work that well, especially when their weed-attracting properties became known away from Hawaii!

Jimmy Lewis then developed the *cut-away* fin, elements of which are still seen on many modern wave fins today. The part of the skeg nearest the board suffers most from turbulence and spin out, so this part is correspondingly cut away, relying on the tip area to provide the grip.

Now skeg design has developed into a major area of board performance. Here we provide a description of the main categories of skeg available:

1. The *pointer* is a popular shape for racing. It provides good lift and upwind ability. With its slightly swept-back tip it offers a broader range and is more user-friendly than the blade fin.

2. The *blade* is a dedicated performance fin that promotes excellent acceleration and top-end speed in fully powered-up conditions. Its tall narrow profile is ultra-efficient but at the cost of manoeuvrability. Using the right size fin for the conditions is vital since they give so much lift that a board can become uncontrollable if 'over-finned'.

3. *Wave* fins come in many forms but their main characteristic is a lower aspect ratio and a swept-back outline shape. They are intended to be easy to use in gybes and help you maintain good grip in extreme conditions. You will often see a cut-away feature and/or a slot in these designs. The slot genuinely helps prevent spin out since pressure difference between each side of the foil can be equalised through the small slit in the fin. Understandably you cannot expect much lift, speed or upwind performance from these fins.

Broadly speaking these cover the options available to you. Many fins are a compromise between these different concepts with the wave/slalom fin being a case in point. Here some of the manoeuvrability features of the wave fin (swept-back shape) are mixed with a higher aspect ratio to create more lift. It is the type of fin that most recreational sailors would be happy with – you just have to consider what length would suit your weight. Heavier people generally need larger fins.

Rail Profiles
(Fig 69)

The rails of your board determine how well it sails upwind and its ability to maintain grip at speed on a reach and during a turn. To do this they work together with the other design features of a funboard.

The rail shape gradually changes throughout a board's length; unless you look carefully it is difficult to see the subtle changes involved. Different rail shapes release the water that is flowing under the board in different ways. For instance, the smooth flowing curve of the soft rail encourages water to follow the line of the rail up around the board, therefore having the effect of sucking the board into the water. This is very good for grip and

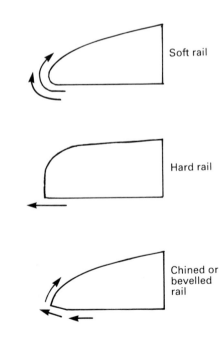

Soft rail

Hard rail

Chined or bevelled rail

Fig 69   Rail profiles showing water release.

reduces the chances of spin out whilst not being very fast. It tends to be used in wave boards where good turning is important.

In total contrast, hard rails release water more cleanly and consequently will tend to plane earlier at the expense of not gripping quite so well in the turns. A very thick hard rail, which you can hardly get your hand around, is often used in the mid-sections of a race board where speed is important, since when the board is sailed at a slight angle the thick rail digs in providing more lateral resistance and thereby helping the daggerboard. These thick rails are called slab-sided or box rails and are now a common feature on most boards.

There is also a compromise of the above shapes – chined or bevelled rails. Widely used on modern boards, these are a combination of hard and soft, giving good water release and maintaining grip in turns. These three shapes provide the basis for numerous other permutations in rail profile.

Tail and Outline Shapes
(Fig 70)

In the early stages of board design, manufacturers produced different tail shapes to suit different boards. However, it soon became apparent that the actual *shape* didn't matter that much, it was the volume and width that were the important factors in performance.

Most boards now favour what surfers would call a rounded pintail or squash tail design, which makes high-speed turns possible. The width of the tail is what the designers adjust depending on a board's intended use. Here are a few comparisons between the characteristics of wide and narrow tails.

NARROW TAIL
Advantages Fast and easy to control in high winds and extreme conditions.
Disadvantages Slow to get on the plane.

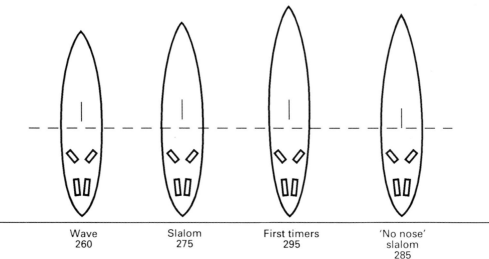

| Wave 260 | Slalom 275 | First timers 295 | 'No nose' slalom 285 |

Fig 70 Comparison between four different types of short board. Note the differences in mast track position in relation to the footstraps.

WIDE TAIL

Advantages   Easy to get planing. Tight slashing turns possible.

Disadvantages   Very difficult to control at speed.

In wave boards wingers are sometimes used as a compromise to provide width at the back of the board for early planing and jumping, while the narrower part towards the tail means control should not be lost at speed.

The overall outline shape of boards also varies depending on the intended use. The wave board will normally be relatively short (less than 2.65m) and fairly wide (55–7cm) in relation to its length. This produces a very curvy outline, which is fantastic at turning. At the other end of the scale, a board intended for more all-round use and for first-time short boarders would be 2.75m+ in length with good volume in the tail to make sailing in marginal conditions easier. As explained in chapter 1, the volume figures are important here since it will illustrate how 'easy' and stable a board is to sail.

A recent design trend at the performance end of the market has been a move towards outline shapes whose centre of maximum width is much further back.

Such designs have been called 'egg'-style boards. This shape drastically reduces the volume in the nose of the board and this means there is less nose area bouncing around in strong winds. With more width towards the tail these boards are lively and responsive to sail but are not recommended for the inexperienced.

The Rocker Line

Perhaps the reason that tail shapes have wrongly received so much attention in the past is that they are the most obviously visible difference between boards. The rocker line, though, which is the most important part of board design, is difficult to identify.

Not only do all boards have a lifted nose, but also a subtle rise in the tail. It is the nature of this curve between nose and tail – the rocker line – that determines a board's speed and manoeuvrability. Racing and speed boards are built with minimum amounts of nose and tail lift, giving long flat areas underneath which are good for speed. However, such boards are difficult to turn and in large waves can nosedive, so for a more manoeuvrable design the rocker line would be made more curved.

5
Advanced Funboard Technique

Once you can carve gybe and water start with ease, you can move on to the more advanced funboard skills. A good level of fitness is needed for this stage since you will often be sailing in Force 5+ winds. Sailing in these conditions also needs an alert awareness of safety matters: you should pick your sailing venues with great care and always sail with others.

Improving Your Gybes
1. Always try to gybe in the gusts.
2. Place your back hand further down the boom before initiating the turn. This will help you sheet in through the turn.
3. Bear away considerably and let the board gain full speed before swaying your weight on to the inside rail.
4. Hunch your shoulders forwards to keep the weight on your toes.
5. Always try to use the flattest stretch of water you can find. This will often be at low water at coastal venues.

The techniques and skills that follow can be performed on all funboards but are best suited to boards under 3.20m as they are more controllable in strong winds.

THE CARVE GYBE ON SHORTER BOARDS

There are subtle differences between gybing long and short boards.

Foot and Body Position

Fig 62 showed the variables in foot placement, indicating that for smaller boards the foot is placed slightly further forwards. To this general rule we can add another variable – the rocker line of the board. For instance, on a fast slalom type board, with only a little tail lift, the foot will have to be placed further back than on a wave board where the rocker line resembles a banana. Each board has slightly different turning characteristics so when trying a new board it takes a while to learn where to put the back foot.

The body position differs slightly by having greater knee bend, since the speed of the board is so much greater. In extreme winds (Force 6+) you have to keep very low to avoid being thrown over the front.

Timing
(Fig 72)

The greatest difference between gybing

Fig 71 Stuart Sawyer carve gybing a
short board at speed. Notice how much
knee bend he uses. Look also at the
position of the rig – in high speed turns
on flat water the sail is deliberately
sheeted in and inclined into the turn.
This makes it easier to lean your
weight into the turn and it is even more
exaggerated when you turn on a wave
face. This technique is also used in
slalom racing.

long and short boards, though, is in the
timing since the short board is travelling
faster and is more sensitive to weight
movements than a longer board. If you try
moving the feet before changing the rig
you are asking for trouble, since in doing
so the board will lose vital speed and normally drop off the plane in the crucial final
stages of the gybe. It is essential, therefore, to release the rig initially and change
the foot positions once sheeted in on the
new course, going strap to strap.

The greater speed enables the rig to be
released earlier. Provided the speed is
good it can be released in the downwind
position, relying on the board's momentum to finish the turn. As your rig changes
improve you should try going from boom
to boom. This misses out the mast since
your hands are placed on to the opposite
boom after releasing; this improves
smoothness and speed.

The timing of the turn is particularly
important in anything other than dead flat
water, since the slope of even the smallest
wave can be used to bank off, therefore
helping to maintain speed. The aim is to
gybe just before an oncoming wave, thus

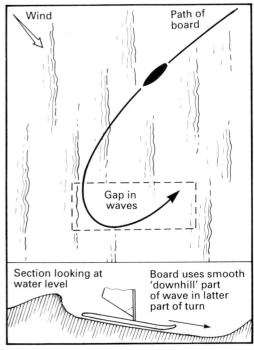

Fig 72 Timing when and where to
gybe in choppy conditions. You should
turn just in front of a wave to make use
of the slope it offers. The bigger the
gap between the waves, the better.

using the 'downhill' part of the wave when you are most vulnerable, i.e. during the latter part of the turn.

Good timing of the turn makes an enormous difference, especially in choppy water. You tend to find that you become accustomed to the timing on your local water and that when sailing in a different place it takes a while to learn the timing of a different wave pattern.

Before moving on to tackle the other types of gybe, you should aim to perfect the standard carve gybe with a success rate of nine out of ten.

THE SLAM GYBE

The slam gybe is a short board version of the flare gybe but without daggerboard and is a useful technique to have in your repertoire. The board spins around on the tail with some assistance from the rig. It is particularly useful when you want to gybe without losing valuable way downwind, for example, when working upwind on a short board or gybing in tight situations such as in front of an oncoming wave or obstacle.

Tips

FOOT PLACEMENT
For a tight turn the back foot will need to be placed a long way back on the board.

BODY POSITION
All the weight has to be used to make the tail dig in, so the posture needed is exactly that of a very bad carve gybe, i.e. straight front leg, leaning back and pulling the rig towards you. Throughout the turn you must keep very low.

SPEED
If you enter the turn at full speed the board will just bounce out of control as you lean back. You need to head into wind slightly to lose speed, before you initiate the turn.

RIG
The rig is partly used to steer the board through the turn by angling it across the board into wind. The rig change is done at the very end of the turn, which will involve a few seconds of clew first sailing.

KILLING THE TURN
To stop the board from turning too much and possibly heading into wind, the turn can be stopped by swiftly moving forwards on the board.

Laydown Gybes

The cover photo of the book shows Peter Hart going into a laydown gybe. This is a high-level type of turn developed from slalom racing. When the board is travelling near to top speed full commitment is needed on the inside edge. The back hand is slid back on the boom, sheeted in and the mast tip is placed into the turn laying down the rig. This allows full upper body angulation into the turn and effectively takes the power out of the sail. Imagine the apparent wind as you go into a turn at 30 knots; as you turn downwind the wind will start blowing straight at you, so it makes sense for the sail to be tucked out of the way. It also looks fantastic since, if performed well, you exit the turn at very high speed; if you try it you'll find the rig change a real handful.

THE DUCK GYBE
(Figs 73 to 77)

This has no practical purpose but is rather a measure of ability – if you can duck gybe you must be quite good. It is a standard carve gybe where instead of letting the sail rotate around the front of the board it is deliberately thrown overhead, involving a 'duck' underneath the sail. When performed well, as well as looking good, it produces a sense of well-being as you smoothly come out of the turn at speed.

The duck gybe can be performed on any board provided that the rig is not too large and the foot of the sail is not too low, for example on racing sails.

It is essential that before you attempt to duck gybe you can carve gybe well, as the feet and body positions are exactly the same. The most important ingredient is speed, since the faster you are going the lighter the rig will feel in the duck (apparent wind). Also, at speed the board is more stable.

Tips

TIMING

This will depend on the wind strength, but as a general rule the hand movements should start about a third of the way into the turn when the board is travelling at its fastest. The stronger the wind, the later you release the rig. Trial and error is the best way to learn the timing, and most people discover that it is better to release sooner rather than later.

KEEP VERY LOW THROUGHOUT

If you are too upright there is a tendency to sway back on to your heels to avoid the boom end. Also, at the end of the turn when the boom is grasped unless you are low you will be pulled straight over as the power comes on.

THROWING THE RIG BACK

When in the position shown in Fig 75, the rig must be thrown vigorously back over your head. A good guide is to try and

THE DUCK GYBE

Fig 73 Duck gybe hand movements. From a normal sailing position with hands equally spaced either side of the balance point (marked by tape), the back hand (B) slides down towards the end of the boom. This will lessen the sudden jolt in the rig as it falls away when the front hand (F) is released.

Fig 74 F releases and crosses over to grasp the end of the boom. Once it has a grip, B releases and passes under the sail to . . .

Fig 75 . . . reach forwards on the new side of the boom. Meanwhile F pulls back sharply over the shoulder.

Fig 76 From a different angle: B is aiming to grasp in front of or as near to the balance point as possible. The lower you duck and the harder F pulls back, the better chance there is of getting well forwards on the boom.

Fig 77   Robby Naish in the latter stages of a duck gybe. He is about to throw
the rig back over his head and momentarily will have no hands on the boom
until his front hand grips. Look at the bend in his left knee: it is an indication of
how crouched and low you should be. If you are anything near upright, the
prospect of a face full of boom or sail causes you to lean back which
completely spoils the turn.

brush your ear with your shoulder as it
throws the rig.

**GRASPING THE BOOM ON THE NEW
TACK**
The sooner you can get the front arm in
front of the balance point the better, since
you are then in a position to spill wind and
control the rig. Getting the hands forwards might involve a little arm over arm
shuffling along the boom.

FEET CHANGE
There is enough to think about already
without having to worry about the feet so,
as in the short board carve gybe, leave the
feet in the straps until after the rig change.

Exercises

It is well worth while practising the hand
movements on the beach (as in Figs 73 to
76), since there must be no hesitation on

the water. In light winds a good practice is to incorporate the duck gybe into the long board flare gybe, this will not only improve the hand movements, but also your sense of timing. The freestyle trick, Sail 360° also uses the same hand movements.

SAILING IN WAVES

Sailing in waves produces an excitement that is difficult to beat and this is partly because it can be slightly dangerous if you are not careful. You must be able to water start with ease and have enough confidence to gybe in front of a breaking wave. Being a strong swimmer is obviously important, as is being reasonably fit, since when a wave puts you through its, 'rinse cycle', you come out disorientated and out of breath.

In true surf conditions only boards of under 3.00m are suitable.

Launching
(Fig 78)

On many beaches this can be the hardest part, as there is often an unpleasant shorebreak. However, this can be a useful built-in safety factor, as it prevents those who aren't up to it from sailing in the waves where they will be a danger to themselves and others.

The beach start is the only way to launch into breaking waves and it needs to be carefully timed. It is worth spending a few minutes looking at how the waves are breaking and picking the best place and time to launch. You should look for the biggest gap between waves; this will probably occur on a gentle slope of the beach, as on a steep part of the beach

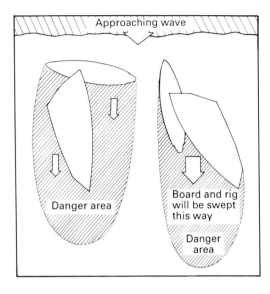

Fig 78a   It is dangerous to be positioned behind the board and rig, because the wave will throw them towards you as it passes.

Fig 78b   Even the smallest of waves contains a frightening amount of power, which can break your body and equipment if you stand in the wrong place.

87

the waves will break closer together. If the wind is blowing directly onshore, you should also work out which is the best tack to set off on.

When you put the board in the water to launch, punch the board through any advancing waves by pushing hard forwards on the rig with one or both hands on the mast. At this stage an important surf rule needs to be observed: *never be in a position directly behind the board or rig as a wave approaches*. Not only is this position dangerous, but it is also the way numerous masts are broken. As the wave washes the board shorewards, the rig resists this movement by digging in and sometimes catching the bottom. The rig cannot stop the force of the wave and the mast breaks. It is always preferable to have the rig nearer the wave rather than vice versa.

Sailing Out

Once you are up and going, you should select your course out through the waves aiming to jump on only one or two waves. To sail over a wave without jumping you need to unhook and let your legs absorb the rising wave – rather like a skier uses his legs like shock absorbers over bumps. Having passed over the wave there is often a tendency to catapult fall, so it is sometimes necessary to sheet out.

The white foamy part of a broken wave is largely made up of air bubbles and the board often digs into it rather than riding over it. When approaching white water you should not have too much speed, sheeting out might be necessary, and the weight should move on to the back foot to encourage the nose to lift over the foam. Anything other than a square-on approach can lead to problems.

Jumping
(Figs 79 to 83)

Jumping is an exciting part of high wind sailing in which there is no limit to the amount you can learn since the possibilities and variation in jumps is endless. Indeed, ten years ago the 360 degree aerial loop was considered an impossible feat but now it is commonplace amongst the top wave sailors. The majority of windsurfers, though, do not enjoy the perfect conditions that are needed to perform such spectacular manoeuvres and we have to make do with much smaller and fewer well-shaped waves.

For your first attempts you should not venture into breaking surf but instead practise 'hopping' off wind-blown chop. Boards with wider tails are more suited to jumping since they will leap off the top of a wave rather than digging into it.

The height and type of a jump will depend on the steepness of the wave and your speed. When sailing in surf it is important to select which wave to jump and also which *part* of the wave face is best. Avoid trying to jump white water, aiming instead to jump at the steepest part of the wave which is normally the part about to break, the critical section.

Air Control
1. Stay crouched and keep the sail sheeted in tightly.
2. When you are in the air use the back foot to pull the tail of the board up under your buttocks. It is this action that levels the board out in flight and makes a small hop into a controlled jump.

JUMPING

Fig 79 *(Above)* Lift off. Launching from the smallest of waves, more lift can be gained by lifting the windward rail thus enabling the wind to catch under the board.

Fig 80 *(Above right)* Now in mid flight, the sail is still sheeted in and the sailor is pulling the back foot under his backside to level off the jump and encourage . . .

Fig 81 *(Right)* . . . a nose first landing. Notice how far back he is leaning to stop the board burying too much.

TIPS

1. Think of all the waves around you as potential ramps from which to launch yourself. With so many potential ramps available, you should look well ahead and select a good steep wave. In this way, rather than it being an impulsive last second decision, you can prepare and focus your attention on what you are about to do.

2. As you approach your selected wave concentrate on getting up as much speed as possible and unhook from your harness. Always try to approach the wave at right angles.

3. As the wave hits the nose of the board, lean back in a crouched position, placing all your weight on your rear foot. This encourages the nose to lift.

4. As the board leaves the wave, use the front foot to lift the windward rail, thereby encouraging the wind to catch under the board and giving more lift.

THE UPSIDE-DOWN JUMP
(Fig 82)

Getting upside-down is far easier than it looks – it just needs the right combination of circumstances. The wave should be very steep to encourage a more vertical flight as you take off. Your speed should not be too great otherwise you will not be able to control the flight of the board in the air. Your weight should suddenly move back as you reach the tip of the wave and you should pull the boom back over your head.

You should aim to dominate your equipment and really 'go for it'. It is probably safer in an upside-down jump to stay with your equipment rather than abandoning it in mid-air since there is the risk of it landing on top of you.

For really extreme positions in the air you can try an angled approach to the wave face. Apparently, in the moments before a 360 degree loop, the board is

Fig 82   An upside-down jump from Robby Naish.

Fig 83   360 degree loops and barrel rolls are now commonplace on Britain's best wave beaches. This shot taken shortly after take-off shows the beginning of the forward gyrating movement that will cause board and rig to spin. For real pose value, why not just take one hand off the boom and do the whole thing one-handed? Landings can often be painful and many 'waveheads' wear protective head and face gear. A face full of boom is not an engaging prospect.

headed into wind so that it takes off from the wave at an oblique angle. Good luck if you try it!

LANDING

Initially it is difficult to avoid falling after a jump. There are, however, three different ways of landing.

1 *The flat landing*   Rather like a belly flop in swimming, this is to be avoided at all costs since the flat impact can break a board in half as well as causing injury to the sailor.

2. *Tail first*   This is the most common landing in the learning stages and provides a much softer option than the flat landing.

3. *Nose first*   As you improve you can develop this landing by lifting the back foot under the buttocks in flight. This is the best of the three since because of the nose rocker the landing is soft and you can recover quickly to the normal sailing position.

If you find that your landings are rather flat, lean back more as you come down.

Riding In
(Fig 84)

In the ideal conditions for wave riding the wind is blowing parallel to the shore but, as with jumping, you can get away with winds that blow slightly onshore. Offshore winds are dangerous and are to be avoided at all costs.

At some stage after you have leapt out through the waves you will need to gybe and hopefully catch a wave back in. There really is no need to sail more than 300m off the beach; remember that the further out you sail the longer the swim back in should your equipment break.

When it comes to riding waves, surfers are the people with the greatest knowledge. You will see groups of them clustered way out beyond the breaking surf waiting for the best waves. These bigger waves arrive in 'sets' of two to five in which the wave height is considerably more than the normal waves. When a set comes through, which may be anything from every five to every forty minutes, the

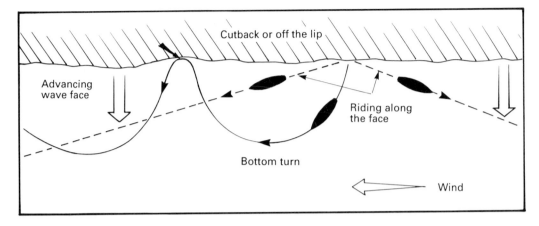

Fig 84   Different methods of wave riding.

more experienced surfers will take the second or third wave of the group since these are normally the biggest. Whilst sailing in surf you should always keep an eye out for these sets since if you don't you may suddenly find yourself amongst large waves whose 'rinse cycles' are considerably more vigorous than that of a washing machine.

Before moving on to the more advanced aspects of wave riding let us consider what should happen in the first attempts.

TIPS

1. As with jumping, you should select your wave well in advance – the only criterion is that it should be fairly small. You should gybe well in front of it and once the turn is completed look behind for your wave. To 'catch' it you might have to slow down and let it come towards you.

2. When the wave approaches, the back of the board will be lifted up and, obeying gravity, the board will shoot off down the slope of the wave. As the tail is suddenly lifted you will need to move your weight back to stop the nose from digging in.

3. As the board accelerates down the face of the wave your speed increases and the apparent wind changes. The sail will need to be sheeted in.

4. To make continued use of slope of the wave it is best to sail along the wave face in either direction, but the favoured direction is that which takes you upwind.

5. Don't get too close to the breaking part of the wave. Get off the wave either by sailing down ahead of it or by slowing down and letting it pass under you.

BEYOND BASICS

As you improve, instead of riding in a straight line along the wave you start manoeuvring by footsteering on the wave just as surfers do. As you catch a wave and accelerate down its face you vigorously steer away from the wind. This is called a *bottom turn* and closely resembles the first half of a carve gybe. However, since the wave is providing all the power for the turn you do not need much power from the rig. So, rather than holding it in front of you as in the carve gybe, you deliberately lose the power from the rig by oversheeting and leaning it towards the wave. As well as losing power this provides support for the pronounced body lean into the turn. The bottom turn should be sharp enough to bring you back up to the top of the wave whereupon you perform what is known as a *cut back* in which you use all your weight on the windward rail to turn the board violently back down the slope of the wave.

Bottom turns and cut backs are performed along the wave leaving a wiggly wake. These more advanced manoeuvres can only be performed in perfect conditions with smooth well-formed waves and a sideshore wind.

Curing Spin Out

Spin out is a far more common occurrence when sailing in waves, since so much air can get under the board. However, waves do not cause spin out on their own; it is partly a result of bad technique.

To cure spin out the aim is to try and spread the sideways force of the sail along the rails of the board, rather than it being concentrated on the straining skeg. One way of doing this is to put the mast track further forwards, thus engaging more of the rail. You can also achieve this by placing some of your weight through the boom to the mastfoot – this is why many top sailors appear to lean forwards with their feet so far back. With feet in the straps, the ankles should be relaxed allowing the sharp leeward rail to bite, which in turn releases the pressure from the skeg. With the skeg placed at the very back, there is also less chance of spin out.

If you do spin out, try recovering by sharply bearing away using footsteering. Otherwise you will have to slow down until the water flow around the skeg re-establishes itself.

Fig 85   Robby Naish watches a competitor perform a one-handed off-the-lip in front of him. If you get caught in one of these breaking waves, it is affectionately known as 'going through the rinse cycle'.

93

6
Competitive Windsurfing

GENERAL POINTS

One of the attractions of windsurfing is speed, and there is no better way to find out how fast you are and improve your technique than racing. It is also an excellent way to meet like-minded people and try out new venues. There is a wide range of standards at which you can compete, ranging from weekly club races to national series events or even international championships. The very pinnacle of the sport is the Olympic Games and the world professional circuit.

Different Classes

At club level the main class is limited by sail size. The most common maximum sail size used is 7.5 sq m, since this is used in some of the international classes explained below. Sometimes heavyweights use an 8.5 sq m sail, but as you can imagine that can become rather specialised and expensive. You will also often find a 6.5 sq m category for newcomers and youngsters. Variations in the precise rules used at clubs are many, but at national level competition normally follows the international classes explained below.

RACEBOARD
This is an open class in which any board and sail may be used provided certain rules are observed. The maximum sail size is 7.5 sq m and nearly all long boards are allowed in this class. Course racing is used in anything from 5–30 knots wind speed. Weight categories are used since body weight is such an important factor; the dividing line between light and heavyweight is 70kg or 11 stone.

ONE DESIGN
A one-design class is one in which all the boards and sails are identical. The most popular class of this type is the Mistral one-design class as the Mistral has been selected as the equipment for the 1996 Olympics. This board is 3.72m long and uses a 7.5 sq m sail; it is also possible to use this board in the raceboard class.

There is another one design for ten- to sixteen-year olds that is particularly popular in Europe. It is the Tiga Aloha, which uses a 6.5 sq m sail.

FUNBOARD
The funboard class has evolved to cater for series production boards of which more than 500 must have been made. There are very few rules governing sails or boards. Official racing only takes place in over 11 knots of wind; this used to mean that long and short boards were used but with the evolution of more efficient equipment, competition now only takes place using short boards. Indeed, specialist course-slalom boards have

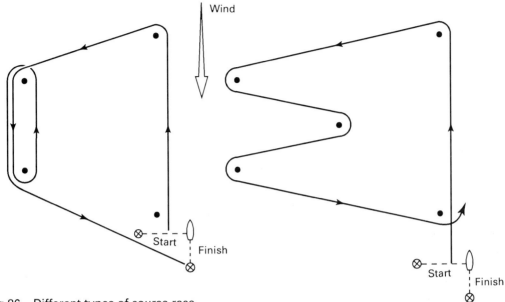

Fig 86   Different types of course race.

been developed for this type of racing along with the standard slalom boards, which are only used in over about 16 knots. Course racing and slalom disciplines are used.

Types of Competition

COURSE RACING
(Fig 86)
This is a race common to all classes, in which the boards race around a set of buoys using upwind and offwind legs.

The type of course varies from class to class. The M-shaped course is widely used in funboard racing where gybing and reaching skills are paramount. Normally a series of races is held and the winner is the person with the least points.

THE SLALOM
(Fig 87)
This takes place in strong winds and only the funboard class use it. It is a test of

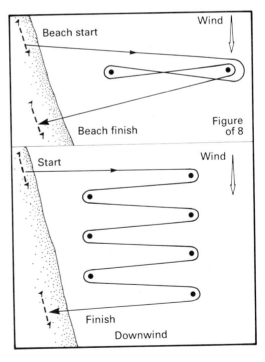

Fig 87   Different types of slalom course.

95

high-speed reaching and gybing and is run in a single elimination heat system with a set number qualifying through to the next round. The start is very important since races normally last less than five minutes.

WAVE COMPETITION

This is only used in the funboard class and in Europe tends to be something of a rarity, as the combination of cross-shore winds with surf is so infrequent. Sailors perform in man-on-man heats in front of a panel of judges, showing off their jumping, riding and turning skills in the waves.

Go-Fast Technique

Before explaining how to tackle a course race it is worth looking at what makes one sailor go faster than another. At local level both slalom and course races can be won by sailing fast without too many tactics. A speed advantage can often make you appear to be a tactical master.

FAST STANCE
(Figs 88 and 89)
On boats the rig is held in position with wire shrouds and top yachtsmen spend many hours tweaking and adjusting their controls for maximum performance. On a board all these fine adjustments are made by our bodies in the way we stand. Here then are the main aspects of a fast stance:

1. *Keep the rig as upright as possible* An upright rig presents more sail area to the wind and keeps the driving force pointing in the right direction – horizontally forwards. This is achieved by using extended arms placed shoulder width apart on the boom. Harness lines should have enough depth to enable the arms to be extended when hooked in.

2. *Keep the sail still, balance using hips and knees* When the sail is sheeted or moved to retain balance, it spoils the airflow around it and wastes valuable power. You should try and keep your balance by moving the knees and hips towards or away from the sail, keeping the shoulders still.

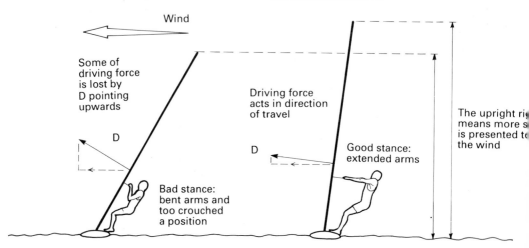

Fig 88   Keeping the rig as upright as possible.

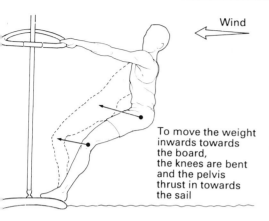

Wind

To move the weight inwards towards the board, the knees are bent and the pelvis thrust in towards the sail

Fig 89   Balancing using the hips and knees (viewed from the front). Notice how the shoulders and arms remain stationary, thus keeping the rig still.

3. *Keep the board level* The board should be sailed in the position it is designed for – horizontal. The exception to this is when you are sailing upwind which will be covered later.

4. *Flex the legs* to absorb oncoming waves. The legs act rather like shock absorbers.

5. *Close the slot* This involves, especially when reaching, trying to close the gap between sail and board. The sail should be rigged with the minimum amount of mast showing at deck level. It is difficult to close the slot in light winds.

6. *Gust response* If you respond to gusts efficiently, without sheeting out to maintain control, you can gain many metres from each gust. To do this you should always be looking upwind to spot the give-away dark furry patches on the water that mark their approach. If the gust looks particularly ferocious then it is worth widening your grip. Crouch low before it arrives and when it hits drop your backside and push your bent legs out to

take the strain. This is an essential skill in gusty offshore winds.

Race Preparation

If you are a newcomer to racing the main preparation is to understand what procedures will be used at the race you are entering. You can learn a certain amount by reading, but the best advice comes from talking to people.

THE EQUIPMENT

The equipment needs to be checked for any signs of wear and tear well in advance, since if anything breaks in a race it is ultimately you who are to blame for not foreseeing it.

Daggerboards and mast tracks should be made to work freely and you should be confident with the non-slip surface. Surfboard wax works wonders for slippery decks. Skegs and daggerboards can be sandpapered to remove any nicks and the uphaul rope can be tied neatly so that it doesn't flap around the ankles in mid-gybe. The slot flusher which closes off the gap on the underside left by the daggerboard case needs to work effectively otherwise, as well as being slowed down, you will have a fountain of water blasting into your face when you go fast.

You will need to wear a watch to time the starts; this should be worn on the wrist of your right hand, with the face on the inside, so that in the final seconds of a frantic starboard tack start it can be easily read whilst in the sailing position.

THE BODY

For top competitors this might involve some form of physical training. In the period immediately before a race it is worth eating something sweet to provide

Fig 90   Speedsailing. Notice how the foot of the rig is closing the slot between board and sail. In some cases a well-designed rig will rest comfortably on the deck and footstraps of the board. Also check out the use of headgear and the use of a number of battens in the sail to provide stability. Speed-orientated sails tend to have a very flat profile shape.

Fig 91   Julian Anderson winning the Marathon (and later the Mistral World Championships) at the age of 17. Notice how after twenty-odd miles of racing his lines have become rather too long, forcing him to sit in his harness to take the weight off his weary arms. Harness lines would normally be a lot shorter these days, but this is a unique picture showing the thrill of success.

glucose and drink plenty of fluids since in a long race you can become dehydrated and can lose up to 5lb. It is also wise to do some stretching and warm-up exercises before launching, especially in strong winds.

THE MIND

This is only of benefit in big events where the skills and fitness of the top sailors are all very similar and it is the state of mind that matters. 'Psyching-up' is what this mental preparation is often called, and for some it starts days before an event. Many people have developed their own ways of preparing themselves, such as rehearsing what they are going to do in their mind. This intriguing subject is covered by an excellent book called *Sporting Body Sporting Mind* (J. Syer and C. Connolly, CUP, 1984) which explains numerous methods of mental preparation.

COURSE RACING

Course racing is used in all the classes and is popular in windsurfing clubs. The main priority at first is to get around the course without falling off; then, as you improve, you can start to think about tactics, some of which are explained below.

The Line Start
(Fig 92)

A line start is the most common method of starting a course race. In simple terms the fleet has to start through an imaginary line usually drawn between a mast and a buoy. A countdown using sound signals together with the raising of flags is given at ten and five, or six and three, minutes before the start, depending on the procedure being used. At one minute before the start a sound signal is made. You can synchronise your digital watch with the countdown to ensure you start exactly as the gun goes.

For obvious reasons, laser beams or submerged fluorescent wires cannot be used to mark the start line. To make sure you are not over the line at the start, try and get an accurate transit – do not use a moving ship on the horizon! It should be checked twice: once before and then again after the second sound signal, since the race team are allowed to move the line between the first and second sound signals. They often do this by letting out or

Fig 92   A line start at the world championships. L190 has a good start in clean air but looks to be at the unfavoured end of the line. 130 and H167 seem to have made good starts, but Z114 better watch out since before long he may be in H167's dirty wind. Meanwhile G120 is facing the wrong way and H131 is in very disturbed wind behind the whole fleet.

WIND

bringing in their mooring line, so keep an eye on them to see which direction they move it in, if at all. It is also worth checking your transit twice, since sometimes the start line drifts in a current before the

Fig 94   Sailing backwards by pushing on the wrong side of the sail – a valuable skill.

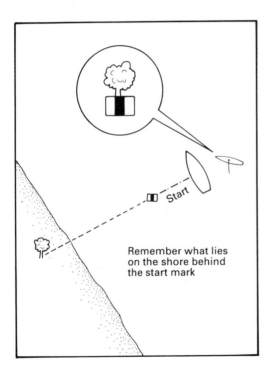

Start

Remember what lies on the shore behind the start mark

Fig 93   Taking a transit from behind the start boat.

anchor grips. At one championship in Barbados they had this very problem, as the buoys needed three hundred feet of line to reach the sea-bed!

BOARD HANDLING
At the start you need very fine control over the board to enable you to manoeuvre into position whilst all the other competitors try to do exactly the same. You need to be able to hold the board in one position without it drifting downwind and also to sail backwards which is invaluable in tight situations.

STARTING TACTICS
(Fig 95)
The first tactical decision is over where on the line you should start. This is determined by the angle the line is set to the

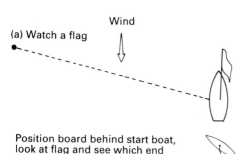

(a) Watch a flag

Wind

Position board behind start boat, look at flag and see which end is closer to the wind.

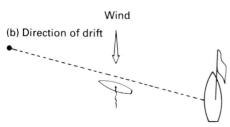

(b) Direction of drift

Wind

Position board along line with sail free. The biased end is the opposite direction to the drift of the board.

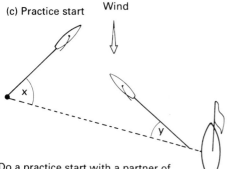

(c) Practice start   Wind

Do a practice start with a partner of equal speed from either end of a line. The favoured end will be that from which the leader sailed. Also, by watching the angle of other boards sailing across the line upwind (i.e. x, y) you can judge the biased end.

Fig 95   Three methods of detecting line bias.

wind, as one end is nearly always better than the other. A line set at exactly right angles to the wind is rare, so you have to set about detecting which is the *favoured end*; three methods for this are shown in Fig 95.

Unfortunately everyone else will be doing the same thing and if one end is blatantly favoured then it is likely to be crowded. Starting at the crowded favoured end is all very well if you can get a good clean start, but more often than not there is so much crowding that only a few boards get away in clean wind. The safer option is to start about fifteen per cent further down the line, thereby giving yourself a little more room.

If the bias towards one end is only small, the best place to start is in the middle where there is often plenty of space and the chances of making a good start are far greater. Most of the top sailors start here, so be careful who you position yourself next to since if they are fast they will soon take your wind.

Tips
1. Trust your watch and accelerate well before the start, do not wait for your rivals to sheet in.
2. When sheeting in to go make sure you are not pointing too high into wind, since the board will not accelerate well if this happens.
3. Above all else try to keep clean wind after the start, even if this means sacrificing pointing angle or even tacking off on to port tack.

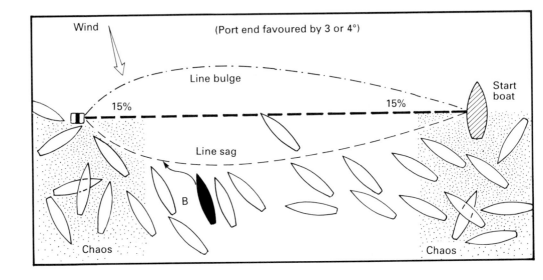

Fig 96   A has remembered his transit and will get a good start well in front of the rest. B is part of the line sag but has kept clear of the chaos within 15 per cent of either end. He has created a gap downwind into which he can accelerate to start at speed, whilst those around him will still be sheeting in.

LINE BULGE AND SAG
(Fig 96)

There is often a large sag in the line-up of boards, because although the people at either end are confident that they are not over the line, the people in the middle can not judge their approach precisely and tend to hold back in caution. If you recognise a sag developing stay confident in your transit and steal an instant lead over your competitors by staying on the line.

In an experienced large fleet everyone is so keen to get a good start that a bulge often forms. This tends to be skewed towards the favoured end and you should aim to be at the front of the bulge.

TACTICS IN THE FINAL MINUTE

So, there you are in the final minute, boards crowded around you and space becoming limited. What you must do is preserve as much of that space as you can, especially downwind of you. As you edge up to the line, keep nudging into wind as this will create a small gap downwind. With between four and eight seconds to go, you can accelerate into this gap, hitting the line at speed whilst those around you are still sheeting in.

The Gate Start
(Fig 97)

The gate start is an alternative to conventional line starting and is sometimes used to start large fleets. The principle is quite simple. A board, whose identity is made known to all competitors, begins sailing upwind on port tack past a buoy in the water about ten seconds before the start gun. Behind this board (called the pathfinder) is the start boat which motors along at the same speed as the board.

102

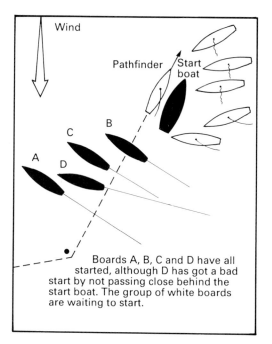

Boards A, B, C and D have all started, although D has got a bad start by not passing close behind the start boat. The group of white boards are waiting to start.

Fig 97   The gate start.

When the start signal goes the boards are free to start by sailing out close behind the start boat on starboard tack. The pathfinder and start boat keep on going until all the fleet have started or for three minutes, whichever is the shorter. At the end of the start the pathfinder tacks and continues to race just like any other board.

In steady conditions this is an entirely fair way to start; a board starting early through the gate has exactly the same chance of reaching the first mark as the last boat through.

A good start is one where you pass close behind the start boat going at speed. The important tactic with this type of start is to decide whether to start early or late in the gates 'opening'. Go late if you want to keep to the right-hand side of the course and early if you want to use the

left side. Also, if you consider yourself to be faster than the pathfinder board, it is worth starting early, since as you wait for him to reach you, you could be sailing that part faster than him. If you consider yourself slower than the pathfinder, then start late.

This is often a good method of starting a small group of boards without a race organiser and it is commonly used in training.

The Upwind Leg

This is easily the most important leg of the course, where a great deal of place changing can go on due to the huge differences in speed between sailors. There are also a large number of tactical decisions to be made as you sail upwind.

TECHNIQUE
Upwind sailing is a part of the sport that many people ignore, concentrating instead on reaching and gybing all the time. It comes as a bit of a shock to some to see how much faster others can sail upwind. There is no magic skill, you just improve with practice.

Your main objective should be to sail as close to the wind as possible whilst maintaining speed. The closer you sail, the slower you go and vice versa. It then becomes rather a compromise of finding the optimum angle to sail to the wind in different conditions. For instance, in choppy water it is worth sacrificing your angle to the wind for a little more speed to punch through the waves.

You can feel if the sail is sheeted correctly by the pressure in the arms (assuming that they are spaced equally about the CE). If the pressure in the front arm decreases then you are sailing too

Upwind Speed
1. Concentrate ruthlessly on always keeping the board pointing high to the wind.
2. Avoid sudden changes in the angle of railing since you will slip sideways every time the water flow is disturbed. Riding the rail smoothly and keeping a consistent railing angle is particularly important in waves.
3. Try to get your feet as far out on to the rail as possible since the further out you are the more leverage you apply to the rig.
4. Keep the rig as still as possible except for pumping out off tacks.
5. If you have an adjustable outhaul pull it fairly hard to create a flat sail with tight leach.

Fig 98   Britain's Olympic windsurfer Penny Way railing the board shortly after the start. By sailing the board at an angle to the leeward rail grips, providing more sideways resistance. The more you push down through your toes and sit in the harness (see fig 34) the more you rail – it's a fine balancing act.

close to the wind. You can practise this skill by deliberately steering a bad variable course and feel the pressure changing in the hands. With practice this skill becomes instinctive and you don't have to think about your sailing – you can just switch yourself to 'automatic pilot' and concentrate on other aspects of the race.

If your arms are fit enough, it is best to sail without using the harness as much as possible since you can make far more sensitive adjustments. In the 1984 Olympics no harnesses were allowed, even in strong winds. Nowadays, though, top sailors use the harness to rest their weary arms on long races.

RAILING
(Fig 98)
On the beat (upwind leg) the board is not sailed level as on all the other points of sailing, but is deliberately heeled to enable the leeward rail to dig in, thus providing more lateral resistance. Indeed, specialised racing boards have rail shapes that are extra sharp. At speed the daggerboard helps to angle the board as Fig 34 showed. Otherwise, the position of the feet along with the amount of weight placed through the booms on to the mast-foot determine the angle of railing. The

optimum angle varies between boards, but it should not be too great or the sideways resistance of the daggerboard is decreased.

TACTICS UPWIND

On the windward leg some of the worst reasons for tacking are: 'It's about time I did one.' 'This left arm's aching too much, I'll have to do one.' 'The sun's gone behind the sail, I'll have to tack.' 'I'll just tack and see how Jim is getting on.' We have probably all used one of these excuses at some stage. However, when you tack it should be for tactical reasons. In club racing you will often tack to avoid 'dirty' wind, whilst at high levels the decisions become more complicated, also involving tidal currents and wind shifts.

AVOIDING DIRTY WIND
(Fig 99)

This is one of the most important things to remember when racing. Dirty wind is disturbed turbulent air behind obstacles (such as trees, buildings and other boards' sails) that greatly reduces a board's speed.

The turbulent wind behind a sail extends about five board lengths downwind and if you are sailing in this area your speed can be as much as halved. However, not only is the wind downwind of a sail affected but also that behind the board, since the sail curves the wind and it takes a few board lengths for it to revert to its normal direction. If you are sailing in this curved air flow you cannot sail as close to the wind as you could if you had been in clear wind. Thus, when racing you are constantly trying to avoid the slowing influence of other boards in search of clear wind.

The importance of getting a good start

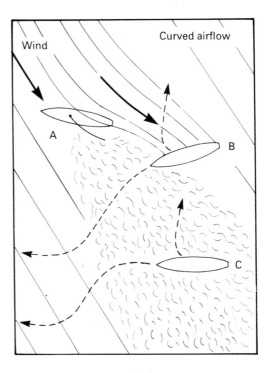

Fig 99 C is sailing in A's dirty wind and must get out of it as soon as possible by either tacking or bearing away. B is sailing in the curved air behind A's sail and cannot point very high. If he stays there too long he will slip into the dirty wind like C, so he must tack off quickly. Both B and C will lose at least four board lengths by sailing in A's influence.

now becomes obvious, since if you fall only a few metres behind in the first minute after the start you fall into everyone else's dirty wind and drop even further back. If you do get a bad start it is worth tacking through the fleet on port tack in search of clear wind. This is very demoralising since you have to pass behind many boards on starboard before getting clear.

Sometimes the boards at the front

seem to extend huge leads over the rest of the fleet. This is not purely a result of them being faster sailors, but partly a measure of the clean wind they have had by being at the front.

When the wind blows off the land you have to consider the effects of trees, hills and buildings. It sometimes proves worth while to tack towards one side of a course to get more wind. These effects are particularly strong on small lakes.

For many people the bible for race tactics is the classic dinghy racing book *Start to Win* by Eric Twiname (Granada, 1975) which clearly explains the complexities of racing tactics. One of his chapters is entitled 'The Beat as an Obstacle Race', which is a good way of thinking about it

since the obstacles to your progress are the numerous areas of dirty wind provided by other sails and you have to do your utmost to avoid them.

WIND SHIFTS
(Figs 100 to 102)

On inland waters and in offshore winds at sea wind shifts can play an important part on the upwind leg. If you tack at the right time, when the wind slightly changes in direction, large amounts of ground can be made over those who are oblivious to the shift. The skill is in spotting these slight changes in the wind. When sailing upwind, a change in the wind direction will either make the board point higher or lower than previously. If you have to

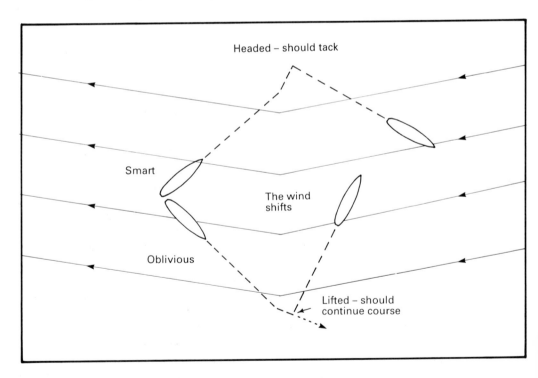

Fig 100   Wind shifts. Oblivious should not have tacked here since he loses out to Smart.

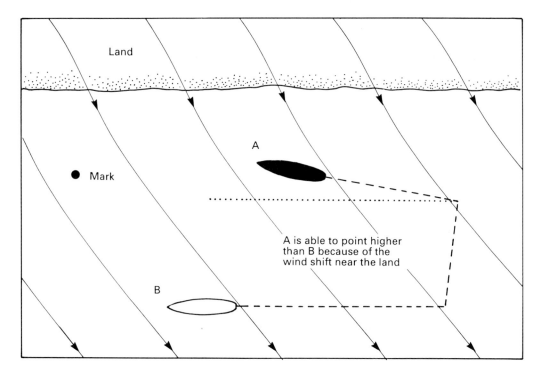

Fig 101   The wind bends at the shoreline in an offshore breeze and tries to cross it at 90 degrees. By sailing towards the land first you will find more favourable wind which will enable you to benefit over those who don't.

point lower because the wind has changed direction (you have been headed), this is a sign to tack and gain ground over those who haven't spotted it.

Recognising the header needs good concentration and confidence. There are, however a few indications that a header has just passed:

1. Front arm loses pressure, sail feels lighter.
2. Need to recover from falling backwards.
3. Loss of speed.
4. Need to push rig forwards and bear away to keep moving.

If all these occur it is a fairly good indication that you should tack.

A useful method of detecting changes in the wind direction is to make a mental note of the point on the shore towards which you are sailing and use this as a reference point. If there is a wind shift you will then point in a slightly different direction.

It really is no use following the tacking pattern of someone who is meant to be good, since the shifts affect different parts of the course at different times. Also, even world class sailors only get it right about 80 per cent of the time, so by following someone you will never beat them and you will often get led the wrong way.

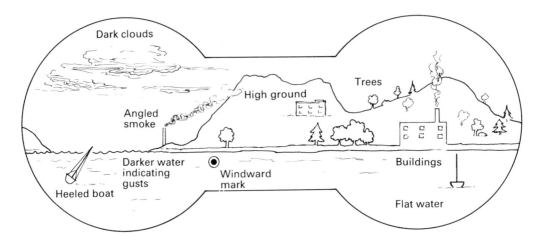

Fig 102   Looking upwind for clues. Here the left side seems to be favoured.

The wind shifts mentioned so far are small and fairly frequent so hopefully you can tack on the headers all the time. But this is by no means the only kind of shift. Sometimes the wind swings steadily round over a period of time, and at other times it blows steadily in a curve. A hill or valley can often act in the same way as an enormous sail and bend the wind over a large area.

Such large wind shifts are important when sailing long upwind stretches. Other than in large championship races, windsurfers tend to use fairly short beats so their influence is decreased. There is, however, one general rule which uses the wind bend principle: *when sailing upwind head for the shoreline side of the beat first.* The advantage of heading towards the shore has to be weighed against the possible disadvantage of lighter winds closer to shore because of the slowing effect of the land. When sailing in offshore winds, however, this rule is more often than not proved right, particularly in coastal bays.

With experience you can sometimes spot the favoured side of a beat by looking upwind for clues. The shape of the land and the potential wind barriers often indicate which side will have more wind. Smoking chimneys display the wind's strength and direction, whilst on the water the behaviour of other sailing craft can do likewise. The darkness of the water will give a clue as to the wind's strength, and an ominous grey cloud usually signals oncoming wind.

TIDAL CURRENTS
(Fig 103)

These can be particularly important on the sea where the tide is not just limited to movements up and down but also to currents which flow in and out of bays and estuaries. There are plenty of clues as to which way the tide is flowing other than tide tables. Moored boats with deep keels (i.e. not motor boats) swing with the current, and you can also detect the flow around buoys. If you know the direction of flow, if it is favourable you obviously benefit by sailing in it, otherwise you should concentrate on keeping out of the

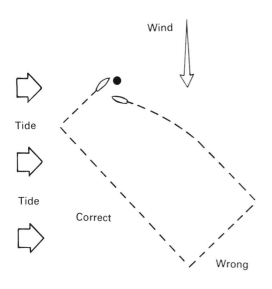

Fig 103   By making the first of two tacks into tide it is easier to judge when to tack for the mark since you are much closer to it than if you take the other course.

flow. Avoiding an unfavourable current can often be done by tacking close to the shore since the water is normally slower when moving at shallower depths. In bays, the tide tends to flow around the bay in one direction as it rises and then reverses as it falls.

An important rule when beating into a current flowing across the upwind leg is always to sail the tack that takes you uptide of the mark first. By doing this you are making it far easier for yourself to judge exactly when you should tack for the mark, since if you take the other tack it is difficult to judge how much the current will sweep you down.

There are, therefore, a number of factors involved in choosing a course to windward. Tactics play a secondary role to board speed; many a race is won by the sailor who is fast off the line and avoids dirty wind enough to use his speed advantage.

Rounding the Top Mark
(Fig 104)

With the whole fleet converging on the first mark it can often get rather chaotic, as everyone is eager to blast off on to the reach. Since starboard tack has right of way the starboard approach is particularly busy, with a line of boards queuing to go round. The perfect line on to which you would tack to make the mark is called the layline. To avoid sailing in dirty wind everyone has to tack slightly late and the queue stacks up above the layline. If you get on the layline too early then you risk being slowed by everyone tacking in front of you and, furthermore, if the wind shifts you have no option other than sailing on, thereby losing ground to your competitors. If you are feeling particularly adventurous you can try approaching on port tack, gambling on being able to find a gap to tack into. In large fleets where there is so much dirty wind on the layline this is often the best tactic.

A point to note about technique is that when you actually go round the mark in strong winds the daggerboard should be retracted first *then* the mast track moved back in preparation for the reach. This way you can accelerate into the reach without the fear of a capsize fall.

The Reach

PUMPING
This is an important skill which helps you to go faster on the reach. It involves sharply pulling the sail towards you

109

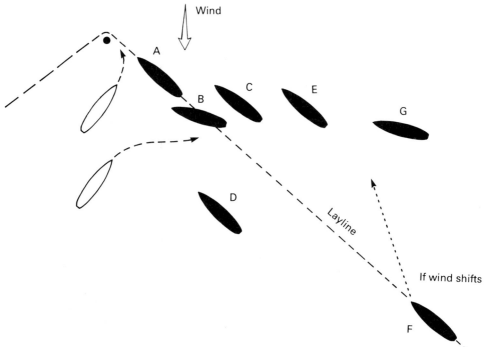

Fig 104 A and C are well placed but E has lost out by being further back in the queue. B is in trouble since he is in dirty wind and cannot tack because C is blocking him. G has completely misjudged the approach by sailing too far above the layline. F has joined the layline too early and as well as getting dirty wind as he approaches the mark, he will have no option but to sail on if there is a favourable shift. The white boards are taking a risk by approaching on port, but they do benefit by sailing in clear wind.

which, for an instant, creates more wind and hence more power. It takes considerable practice to perfect and if done badly slows you down rather than speeding you up. The signal to pump is when the back of the board is being lifted by a wave. The important part of pumping is the timing relative to the wave. You should always pump at the top of the wave as the board is about to accelerate down the face. This timing is vital even on the smallest of waves since if you pump at the bottom of a wave you will not go any faster.

Pumping at the highest level, such as at the Olympics, is extremely demanding on the body. Shoulders, elbows and lower back are all vulnerable to injury if you are not fit enough for the job. Obviously on lighter wind reaches it is not just down to how fit you are but also how much you want to win – pumping full on can hurt. Of course, in the past pumping was not permitted within the rules because people felt the sport would become too physical.

It is also very useful to practise pumping straight downwind on a run. It is beyond the scope of this book, but uses a type of scooping, rowing action.

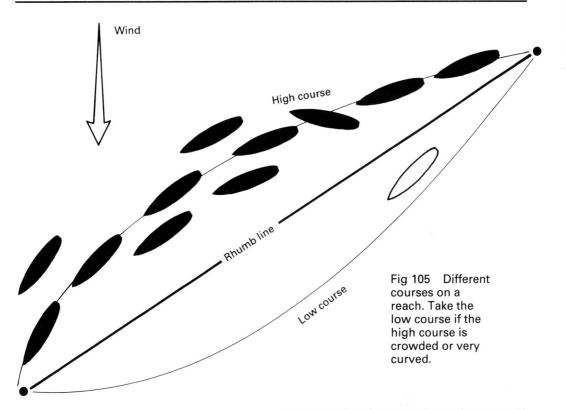

Wind

High course

Rhumb line

Low course

Fig 105 Different courses on a reach. Take the low course if the high course is crowded or very curved.

REACHING TACTICS
(Fig 105)
Again, the main tactic is to avoid dirty wind. This will mean you have to steer a slightly bowed course to discourage others from passing to windward. If the reach is fairly broad the fleet often steers a very curved course to the next mark, so it is sometimes worth deliberately keeping well clear on a low course.

If there is a tide flowing, to avoid being swept downtide you can take a transit on the next mark to steer the rhumb line.

Reaching Speed
1. In planing conditions maintain a locked out position in which you never sheet out. Let most of the weight go through the harness.
2. Always look ahead looking for the best path through the wave troughs.
3. Avoid pumping *uphill* on the back of waves.
4. Any adjustable outhaul should be loosened to create a fuller loose leach shape.

Tactics at the Gybe
(Figs 106 and 107)

If you are rounding without any boards near you, you should aim to approach the mark wide and come out close, this tactic

is known as 'in wide-out close'. This way no valuable ground is lost to windward at the end of the turn and it 'shuts the door' on anyone trying to make a furtive inside rounding. The in wide-out close principle

111

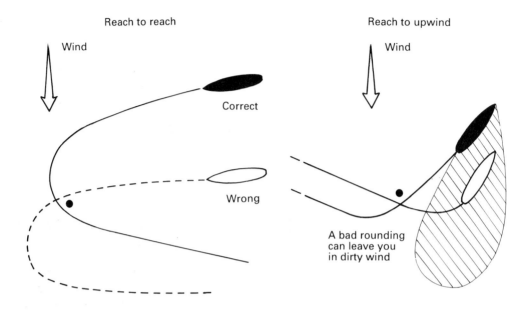

Fig 106 'In wide-out close.'

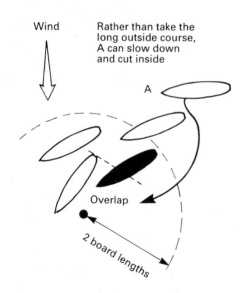

Fig 107 Rounding with others. Remember: you can only ask for water if you establish and maintain an overlap before you are two board lengths from the mark.

has particular importance at the bottom mark, since the following leg is to windward and a bad rounding can result in dirty wind at the outset.

Rounding in the company of others is a different matter, as you can use the rules to help you. If you are the inside board and have an overlap over a board outside you at two board lengths before the mark, you are entitled to the inside position around the mark, that is, space to round; this is called 'water' at the mark. This means that you should always aim to approach the mark on the inside of other boards, even if it means altering your course down the reach. Provided you get an overlap you can shout 'water' and the other boards have to give you space to gybe in.

Strange though it may seem, it sometimes pays to slow right down before rounding. When a bunch of boards rounds the mark, rather than get forced wide with the group and risk the possibility of a rig being dropped in your path, you can slow up and coolly take an inside rounding.

Winning

The person who wins races is usually experienced. Experience heightens our powers of observation since it teaches us what to look for. The winner is busy searching the water, nearby boards, the sky and shore for every scrap of race-winning information. He concentrates every second on the race because he has more than enough to concentrate on. However, the information the tail-ender picks up is probably less than half of what the expert picks up. Armed with inadequate information he usually fails to see why one moment is better for putting in a tack than any other. He isn't sure of what he should be looking for, so he doesn't look and his mind is therefore fairly free to contemplate subjects unconnected with windsurfing.

To be able to concentrate so fully on a race needs good boardhandling skills, since you shouldn't have to think about how to sail the board fast, it should have become instinctive. It is only when sailing the board fast has become natural that the attention can be fully focused on tactics. So, it doesn't need the rigorous coaching of, for example, athletics to improve, merely plenty of time on one board learning how it behaves.

When it comes to sailing in a series of races the emphasis must be on consistency. You don't have to finish first in each race, merely in the leading group. Consistent sailing means not taking too many unnecessary risks, such as not starting at the crowded end of the start line or

---

Winning Tips
1. Know your equipment inside-out so that you can totally dominate it.
2. Be well prepared physically, as well as in your knowledge of conditions and the racing procedures to be used.
3. Time spent sailing on the water is the key.

---

sailing completely to one side of the beat where just one unfavourable wind shift can ruin you.

Avoid being involved in a protest at all costs since not only does it risk a disqualification, but it also ruins your concentration as you ponder over the incident. I was involved in a protest in the morning race of a world championship and the hearing was not until later that evening. My result in the afternoon race was the worst of the event as I dwelt over my fate up the first beat. By sailing consistently over a series of races, you win by other people's mistakes.

SLALOM RACING

Slalom racing is usually held in strong winds, so it is fast, exhilarating and good to watch. Unlike the course race, the start is off the beach and the course has no upwind leg so shorter boards without daggerboards are used. It complements course racing, since when conditions are too severe to lay a course offshore the slalom competition can be run within 200m of the beach, with marks being laid by wading into the surf. With boards travelling at up to 25 knots, the emphasis is on not falling since in a few seconds the fleet will have zoomed past and gained a huge advantage.

A series of heats are held, usually with the first four boards going through to the next round, culminating in a final. Each heat lasts for about three to five minutes, with the final often being a series of three races. If time permits the heats are arranged on a double elimination or league basis whereby you have to lose more than once before being eliminated.

The Beach Start

With a beach start everyone is allocated a position on a short line on the beach, the race organiser checks everyone is ready and then signals the start. This is often the decisive part of the race, since if you launch well and get clear of the group it is only your own mistakes that will stop you from qualifying.

The skill is in running down the beach with all your equipment, often in a stiff breeze. Everyone develops their own favourite method, but you must be able to run, keeping the board and sail from blowing all over the place. Whilst doing this you need to avoid the other competitors. Before the start, just let them know you are there and don't let anyone crowd you; make as much space for yourself as you can. If you have drawn an end position on the line, run down the beach a little wide to give yourself more room.

As you approach the water put the board in deep enough not to rip the skeg out and push the board a little further out using one hand on the mast. If you use both hands on the boom to run through the shallows it will only need an awkward gust or wave to rip the sail from your grasp. With the hand on the mast control is far easier.

Fig 108   Top British lightweight sailor Howard Plumb cranking his 3.72m raceboard with 7.5 sq m sail into a turn. Notice how even on this length of board all the features of a slalom-style gybe are present: low body position and over-sheeted sail leaning into the turn. The extended front arm keeps the weight forward and will create space for him when he comes to change the rig.

The Race

Having launched and got going you should be attacking, going fast and trying to pass others in an effort to get clear wind. Fast technique has already been covered earlier in this chapter. An added speed factor is the way in which you go over the waves – just like a ski racer, the

Fig 109   Robby Naish gybing in a Force 6 or 7 slalom race. In this wind he
dare not extend his front arm since he may get pulled over, so instead he is
crouching low and leaning slightly forwards which achieves the correct upright
rig effect. Since the true wind is so strong, the apparent wind plays little part.

longer you spend in the air the slower you go. So you need to anticipate and absorb each wave with the legs (which act as shock absorbers). A further way of avoiding too much time in the air is to lift the back foot as you go over a wave, this helps to stop the nose lifting. Also, as you take a wave try to avoid sheeting out since you lose valuable power.

In slalom the turning rules of conventional course racing do not apply. The priority is with the person who leads going into a turn. Protests are uncommon here since it is in each sailor's own interest to avoid high speed collisions which not only ruin your chances but can be quite dangerous. On the gybes the aim is not to fall in and to keep clear of others. If you can do an in wide-out close turn it is a bonus. In large surf it is sometimes worth slowing down and letting a large wave pass before attempting the gybe.

Having established a position you can consolidate it by using defensive tactics to keep other boards behind you. Heading up high means that it is difficult for anyone to pass since you can always bear away down on to them, forcing them to sail in your dirty wind. Also, when bearing off your speed increases dramatically.

115

The beach finish either involves getting you and your equipment through the line or more commonly just yourself.

OTHER DISCIPLINES

Pursuit Racing

This is not really a separate discipline, just another way of running a race. For many people it is rather demoralising to finish a long way behind the leaders all the time and so pursuit racing is an attempt to provide a handicapping system. A fairly small course is needed with an upwind leg. The handicaps are worked out on the results of a trial race and then on all subsequent races everyone starts at minute intervals depending on their previous result. The least able sailors start first and then a minute later the next group start and so on, finishing with the best sailors who often have a handicap of 10 minutes on a 25-minute race. The aim is for everyone to finish together.

After each race the handicaps are altered accordingly, so there is personal satisfaction in decreasing your handicap much the same way as in golf. This system has proved popular with club racing enthusiasts.

Speedsailing
(Fig 90)

In the early 1990s windsurfers continued to shock the world with ever increasing speeds over 45 knots. This is an astonishing speed of over 50 m.p.h. Speedsailing is now a very specialised pursuit since the very fastest times have been set at only one, custom-built venue. Yes, it is actually a constructed piece of water

known affectionately as 'the Ditch'. In the south of France at St Maries de la Mer a canal has been dug at about 120–130 degrees to the Mistral wind, which often blows in the spring of each year. You can only sail one way on it when it is being used; Jeeps are used to ferry the equipment back to the other end of the 500m course.

In England, Weymouth, once the doyen of speedsailing, is now considered too rough to achieve high speeds on and the two most popular venues are West Kirby and The Ray (Southend).

To reach these high speeds very narrow boards, which are often less than a foot wide, are used with specialised camber induced sails. Recently, production boards have shown that they too can exceed 40 knots.

Freestyle
(Fig 110)

Freestyle is a form of trick sailing where the sailor performs a routine in front of a panel of judges, similar to ice skating or gymnastics. It is an excellent way of improving your windsurfing skills, as you learn how the board behaves in all sorts of weird situations.

One of the classic freestyle skills is rail-riding where the sailor flips the board on its side and sails along, coolly standing on the edge. Another of the skills incorporated into a freestyle routine is the pirouette, in which the sailor lets go of the rig and spins round once or twice before catching it again. In competition a sailor has to perform a three-minute routine, performing as many tricks as he can and linking them together with a smooth flowing act. *Dee Caldwell's Book of Freestyle Boardsailing* (Fernhurst Books, 1983) provides a good explanation as to what is involved.

Variations

TANDEMS

Sailing a two-man board is great fun since not only is it particularly fast in moderate winds but there is also the uniqueness of being able to share your exhilaration with someone else. It might not be worth buying a two-man board, but if you ask around you will often find one lying unused in a backyard. They need flat water to perform well and on no account should they be taken into waves since not only are they difficult to manoeuvre well but they are also liable to snap because of their length.

Steering is largely done by one of the sailors sheeting out, for instance, if the back sail is depowered the board will bear away with all the power still on at the front.

If you want a hilarious day's sailing, I strongly recommend the two-man board.

LANDSURFING

The windsurfing concept is not limited to use on the water and in recent years windsurfing sails have been seen on land, snow and ice. The simplest form of landsurfer is a rig attached to a skateboard. This needs a suitably smooth surface and very careful balance as all the steering is done with weight.

The most popular board on wheels, however, has been the speedsail, which is like an enormous skateboard some five feet long with air-filled tyres. The speedsail, because of the very low friction, can do very high speeds in light winds, indeed it is positively dangerous in anything above a Force 2. The 'vehicle' is foot-steered and some have claimed that it has helped their gybing technique tremendously. Do be very careful, though, when having a go since it takes a little getting used to and falls can be very uncomfortable to say the least. There is, in fact, an organisation in France that runs world championships for the speedsail, where tactics are unimportant and it is just a matter of courage as speeds of up to 50 m.p.h. have been recorded.

Even more hair-raising is the thought of landsurfing on ice, which is apparently the winter occupation of some windsurfers in Scandinavia.

Indoor Windsurfing

This was pioneered in Paris where the first ever indoor event was held at the Bercy Stadium. The slalom races are started by launching off a ramp. The wind is supplied by a bank of numerous industrial-size fans on one side of the large indoor pool. These supply a Force 4–5 which is enough for the top pros to get planing on high-volume boards. There is also a jumping competition where competitors take off from a specially constructed ramp – full loops and barrel rolls are performed to the rapturous applause of 15,000 spectators.

It has brought the sport to a far wider audience with live coverage on numerous TV channels worldwide. Other events have been staged in Barcelona and Tokyo. If you want a slice of the action most windsurfing magazines now offer packages to go along and watch the stars in action – it's quite an experience!

Appendix 1

RYA NATIONAL WINDSURFING SCHEME COURSE CONTENT

Guide to Windsurfing Ability	LEVEL 1 Learn to Windsurf	LEVEL 2 Improving Techniques	LEVEL 3 An Introduction to Planing Techniques
LAUNCHING, STARTING AND LANDING	Carrying and launching the board and rig separately; establishing the secure position; coming ashore.	Launching and landing with board and rig connected; introduction to beach starting; securing equipment ashore.	Carrying the board and rig assembled; beachstarting in a variety of conditions; uphauling in stronger winds.
SAILING TECHNIQUES AND STANCE	Sailing across the wind; upwind and downwind; power control; steering; sailing a triangular course.	Improved stance on all points of sailing; basic harness technique; using the daggerboard.	Harness and line adjustment; stance in harness; using the 'training straps'; planing stance; using the mast track.
MANOEUVRES	Turning the board around; basic tacking and gybing.	Improved tacking and gybing; effects of weight distribution.	Tacking in stronger winds; gybing exercises; gybing in a variety of wind strengths, with and without the daggerboard.
SAILING THEORY	Points of Sailing; the 'no go zone'; how a board steers; sailing a course.	How the sail works, the centre of effort; sail tuning; sailing close-hauled, the centre of lateral resistance.	Apparent wind effects; railing upwind; mast track usage; planing technique.

LEVEL 4	LEVEL 5	LEVEL 5
Planing Techniques	**Advanced Planing Techniques – Short Boards**	**Advanced Planing Techniques – Long Boards**
Launching and coming ashore in small waves; variations for board size; water start exercises; rig recovery; the water start.	Alternative methods of carrying; beach starting in waves; uphauling short boards; clew first and light wind water start.	Carrying long boards in different wind conditions; beach starting in strong winds; uphauling large sails; water starting in a variety of conditions.
Key points of planing technique; stance exercises; closing the slot; speed; use of footstraps, mast track and harness to best effect.	Refinements in stance to suit water state; controlling excessive power; sailing in waves; jumping and wave riding.	Refinements in stance on all points of sailing; stance when overpowered; effective use of mast track; railing.
Tacking shorter boards; non planing gybes; carve gybe exercises and progressions; the carve gybe on a variety of boards.	Short board carve gybe; slalom gybe; duck gybe; slam gybe; tacking shorter boards.	Displacement gybes; carve gybe variations; duck gybe; helicopter tack; advanced tacking.
Speed, the theory; sails, the advantages and disadvantages of different types; spin out, causes and solutions.	Types of jumps and landing; leach twist; apparent wind and waves; physical and mental preparation.	Relationship between board, sail and skeg size; leach twist; physical and mental preparation.

Appendix 2

THE BEAUFORT SCALE OF WIND FORCE

Beaufort No.	General Description	Sea Criterion	Landman's Criterion	Limits of* velocity in knots
0	Calm	Sea like a mirror.	Calm; smoke rises vertically.	Less than 1
1	Light air	Ripples with the appearance of scales are formed, but without foam crests.	Direction of wind shown by smoke drift but not by wind vanes.	1 to3
2	Light breeze	Small wavelets, still short but more pronounced. Crests have a glassy appearance and do not break.	Wind felt on face; leaves rustle; ordinary vane moved by wind.	4 to 6
3	Gentle breeze	Large wavelets. Crests begin to break. Foam of glassy appearance. Perhaps scattered white horses.	Leaves and small twigs in constant motion Wind extends light flags.	7 to 10
4	Moderate breeze	Small waves becoming longer; fairly frequent white horses.	Raises dust and loose paper; small branches are moved.	11 to 16

Beaufort No.	General Description	Sea Criterion	Landman's Criterion	Limits of* velocity in knots
5	Fresh breeze	Moderate waves, taking more pronounced long form; many white horses are formed. Chances of some spray.	Small trees in leaf begin to sway. Crested wavelets form on inland waters.	17 to 21
6	Strong breeze	Large waves, taking form; the white foam crests are more extensive everywhere. Probably some spray.	Large branches in motion; whistling heard in telegraph wires, umbrellas used with difficulty.	22 to 27
7	Near gale	Sea heaps up and white foam from breaking waves begin to be blown in streaks along the direction of the wind.	Whole trees in motion; inconvenience felt when walking against wind.	28 to 33
8	Gale	Moderately high waves of greater length; edges of crests begin to break into spin-drift. The foam is blown in well-marked streaks along the direction of the wind.	Breaks twigs off trees; generally impedes progress.	34 to 40
9	Severe gale	High waves. Dense streaks of foam along the direction of the wind. Crest of waves begin to topple, tumble and roll over. Spray may affect visibility.	Slight structural damage occurs (chimney-pots and slates removed).	41 to 47

Glossary

Apparent wind   The wind that you experience blowing in your face when moving. It differs in direction and speed from the true wind experienced when standing still.

Balance point   The imaginary point where the CE acts on the boom through which the sail balances.

Battens   Pieces of flexible glass fibre that slot into 'pockets' in the sail which help to create an efficient aerodynamic shape. Full length battens extend right across the sail.

Beach start   A way of starting in shallow water that involves stepping on to the board with the rig already in the sailing position. When using this technique, the rig does not have to be raised from the water.

Bearing away   Steering away from the wind.

Beating   Sailing into the wind by doing a series of zig-zags.

Beaufort scale   A scale of measurement of wind speed based on knots invented in 1805 by Admiral Beaufort. The scale is measured from Force 0 to Force 12.

Blank   A large piece of polyurethene or polystyrene foam which is shaped by hand into a custom board.

Boom   The curved alloy tube covered with rubber that you hold to control the sail.

Bottom turn   The high speed turn at the bottom of a wave which brings you back up the same wave enabling you to continue your ride in.

Broad reach   The direction of sailing which is roughly half-way between a reach and a run.

Camber inducers   Specially shaped pieces of plastic in the mast sleeve into which full length battens slide. They make the front part of the sail considerably more efficient and are primarily used in race sails.

Carve gybe   A gybe performed with the daggerboard retracted in strong winds, in which the board is turned by foot steering with no assistance from the sail.

CE   The centre of effort. The imaginary central point in the sail through which the power of the sail acts.

Centreline   An imaginary line drawn lengthways down the middle of the board.

Cleat   A small fitting used to secure the control lines of the rig.

Clew   The back corner of the sail which is attached to the end of the boom.

Close hauled   The course you steer when beating, i.e. sailing as close to the wind as possible.

CLR   The centre of lateral resistance. The main point about which the board will resist sideways drift and about which it turns. This will be just behind the daggerboard when it is down.

Concaves   A slightly curved shape used on the underside of boards to produce greater speed.

Course racing   A discipline of competitive windsurfing which involves racing around a course marked by a series of buoys.

Critical section   The part of a wave that is about to break.

Cut back   An aggressive manoeuvre in wave sailing, where the sailor suddenly changes course whilst on the face to return to the bottom of the wave.

Daggerboard   This is sometimes called the centreboard. It is a large 'fin' which gives stability and stops the board slipping sideways. In stronger winds it is retracted inside the board.

Downhaul   The line that tensions the sail down the length of the mast and is connected to the mast foot. It controls the shape at the front of the sail.

Dual batten system   A way of indicating that the sail can use full or half length battens.

Duck gybe   A gybe in which, instead of the sail passing around the front of the board, the sailor ducks down and throws it overhead.

Dumping waves   Waves which break vigorously on a steep beach. This commonly occurs at high tide.

Fin   (Also known as the skeg.) The small piece of plastic or glass fibre protruding at the tail of the board which helps to keep it sailing in a straight line.

Flare gybe   A gybe normally performed on longer boards with the daggerboard down. The board is steered through the turn using the rig.

Foot   The bottom edge of the sail.

Footsteering   The use of your weight (feet) to steer the board in strong winds with the daggerboard up.

Footstraps   Straps at the back of the board into which you put your feet when sailing at speed in stronger winds.

Force   A measurement of windspeed using the Beaufort scale.

Freestyle   Performing tricks on a board; sometimes used as a discipline in competitive windsurfing.

Funboard   A board that is easy to sail in strong winds which has a surf-board type of tail, footstraps, a retracting daggerboard and a mast track.

Gate start   A method of starting a race, mainly used for large fleets, in which boards file out behind another board.

Gybe   Turning the board around by steering away from the wind and letting the sail pass over the front of the board.

Harness   A garment worn to take the strain off the arms, which is attached to either side of the boom, by the use of a hook and lines.

Heading up   Steering towards the wind.

IBSA   International Boardsailing Association. The governing body of the Olympic Division II class.

Inhaul   The line that is used to attach the boom to the mast.

IYRU   International Yacht Racing Union. The body which oversees all competitive sailing and windsurfing except Funboard racing.

Knots   Nautical miles per hour. A nautical mile is 2,000 yards rather than the more familiar 1,760, so 10 knots is almost 11½ m.p.h.

123

Leeward   The side of the board that is furthest from the wind. (The opposite to windward.)

Line start   The conventional way of starting a course race using an imaginary line between two designated points, usually a boat and a buoy.

Lip   The 'lip of a wave', i.e. the crest.

Mastfoot   The means of attaching the mast to the mast track.

Mast track   The sliding device that enables the mast foot to be moved up and down the board.

Nose   The front (pointed) end of the board.

Offshore wind   A wind that blows away from the shore.

Olympic triangle   The triangular shaped course used at the Olympics by both boats and windsurfers.

One design   A class in which racing takes place on identical boards and sails.

Open class   A class where racing takes place on boards conforming to a set of measurement rules, i.e. Divisions I and II.

Outhaul   The line that pulls the clew of the sail out towards the end of the boom. It controls the overall curve or 'fullness' of the sail.

Overhand   The grip used on the boom where the fingers point downwards.

Oversheet   This happens when the sail is pulled at too tight an angle to the wind, i.e. when the back hand is pulled in too much.

Plane   To sail at speed, enabling the board to rise up and travel across the water surface rather than pushing the water aside and sailing through it.

Port   The nautical way of saying left. You are sailing on 'port tack' when your left hand is the one nearest the mast.

Pumping   The action of sharply jerking the rig towards you which momentarily creates more wind in the sail and increases speed.

Rail   The edge or side of the board.

Railing   The skill of sailing the board at an angle, allowing the downwind rail to dig in and therefore providing more sideways resistance.

Reaching   Sailing in a direction across the wind, with the wind blowing at or near an angle of 90 degrees to the board's course.

Rhumb line   The line followed when sailing in a fixed direction.

Rig   The collective name for the mast, boom and sail when assembled.

Rip   A strong current, commonly experienced on surf beaches.

Rocker   The overall curve in the board from nose to tail.

Run   The term used to describe the course of the board when sailing in the same direction as the wind.

Secure position   The position across the wind, with the hands on the mast, which you adopt prior to sailing off.

Set   A set of waves is a group of waves which are larger than average.

Sheeting in/out   Changing the angle that the sail makes with the wind by pulling in or letting out the back hand.

Simulator   A land-based board mounted on a turntable device which is used to teach the basics before going on to the water.

Sinker   A very small board which is

used in stronger winds. It is called a sinker because it sinks beneath you when you are stationary.

Skeg   See Fin.

Slalom   A competitive discipline normally held in stronger winds which uses a fast reaching course with numerous gybes.

Slam gybe   Sometimes referred to as a 'scissors gybe'. It is a very tight version of the carve gybe performed on shorter boards, where the board is turned in a short distance.

Slot flusher   A device which aims to make the flow of water over the daggerboard slot as smooth as possible.

Soft sail   A sail which does not use full length battens.

Spin out   A phenomenon which can occur on a high speed reach when air bubbles work their way down the skeg and cause it to lose its grip in the water. The board suddenly slews sideways.

Split batten system   A variation on the camber inducer idea which uses full length battens that split around the mast giving an efficient shape.

Starboard   The nautical way of saying right. You are sailing on 'starboard tack' when your right hand is the one nearest to the mast.

Steamer   A one-piece wetsuit with close-fitting neck, ankle and wrists. A true steamer should use a waterproof 'blind stitch' on the seams to prevent water penetration.

Tack   Turning round by steering into the wind and stepping around the front of the mast.

Tail   The back end of the board.

Tandem   A windsurfer designed for two.

Transit   A method used in racing to judge how near the start line you are.

Trim   The manner in which the board lies in the water. This is determined by where you put your weight.

True wind   The wind that is experienced when you are stationary.

UJ (universal joint)   This is attached to the mast foot and allows the rig to be moved in all directions. This formed an integral part of the first windsurfing patent.

Uphaul   The thick piece of rope that is used to raise the rig from the water.

Upwind   The direction that is into the wind. The opposite is downwind.

Underhand   The grip used on the boom when the fingers point up.

'V'   The underwater shape at the very back of the board.

Volume   The volume of a board determines its buoyancy and, to some extent, its speed in different wind conditions.

Water start   An advanced manoeuvre used in stronger winds in which the sailor lets the sail pull him on to the board from a position in the water.

Windshift   A change in the wind's direction that can either be sudden or gradual. It becomes an important part of tactics on upwind legs as you get to higher standards.

Windsurfer   The first make of board was a 'Windsurfer' invented by Hoyle Schweitzer. Since then the name has become associated with the sport itself in the form of windsurfing.

Windward   The side of the board that is closest to the wind. Opposite to leeward.

Useful Addresses

RYA Windsurfing (general information)
Romsey Road
Eastleigh
Hampshire SO50 9YA
Tel: 0703 629962
Fax: 0703 629924

UK Boardsailing Association
(Raceboard Class Association)
PO Box 36
Sarisbury Green
Southampton
Hampshire

International Mistral Class Organisation
(IMCO)
Unit 3, North Close Business Park
Shorncliffe
Folkestone
Kent CT20 3UH

British Windsurfing Association
(Funboard Class Association)
Mengham Cottage
Mengham Lane
Hayling Island
Hampshire PO11 9JX

POPULAR HOLIDAY CENTRES

Good instruction and equipment hire are available at these centres; the author has been to them all. Those with (R) offer residential facilities.

Berkshire
Bray Lake
Monkey Island Lane
Windsor Road
Maidenhead
Berkshire SL6 2EB
Tel: 0628 38860

Cheshire
Boundary Park Windsurfing
Knutsford Road
Holmes Chapel
Cheshire CW4 8HT
Tel: 0477 534172

Cornwall
Outdoor Adventure (R)
Atlantic Court
Widemouth Bay
Nr Bude
Cornwall EX23 0DF
Tel: 0288 361312

Hampshire
Calshot Activities Centre (R)
Calshot Spit
Fawley
Southampton
Hampshire SO4 1BR
Tel: 0703 892077

Wales
West Wales Windsurfing (R)
Dale
Nr Haverfordwest
Dyfed SA62 3RB
Tel: 0646 636642

Plas Menai National Watersports
    Centre (R)
Llanfairisgaer
Caernarfon
Gwynedd LL55 1UE
Tel: 0248 670964

West London
Queen Mary Sailsports
Queen Mary Reservoir Sailing Club
Ashford Road
Ashford
Middlesex TW15 1UA
Tel: 0784 248881

Abroad
Minorca Sailing Holidays (R)
58 Kew Road
Richmond
Surrey TW9 2PQ
Tel: 081 948 2106

Sovereign Sailing (R)
Centres in Greece, Turkey and Sardinia
Tel: 0293 527772

Index